CREDIT REPAIR

SECRETS

How to Fix Your Bad Credit

On Your Own

Edward Grey

ISBN: 978-1-80283-853-4

"When you get in debt you become a slave."
-Andrew Jackson

TABLE OF CONTENTS

1. INTRODUCTION

Credit repair is the method of restoring bad credit status that has degraded due to many factors. It could be as easy as disputing incorrect details with credit bureaus to improve one's credit standing. Identity theft and the resulting credit loss can necessitate extensive credit repair work.

Another type of credit repair deals with basic financial problems, such as budgeting, and beginning to fix genuine lender concerns.

Credit restoration has always been critical. Mortgage, car, and personal lenders have long relied on your three-digit credit score to decide your creditworthiness. Lenders often use your credit ratings to calculate how much interest you'll pay on these loans. However, lenders aren't the only ones who use credit ratings to make financial decisions. When making hiring decisions, an increasing number of employers use work applicants' credit records. Many with poor credit can miss out on their dream jobs. Even car insurance providers also use credit ratings to determine policy rates. It's obvious that getting a good credit score is the secret to living a stress-free life today.

Nothing a credit repair agency can legally do for you, including deleting incorrect details, that you can't do for yourself for little to no cost. Hiring such a company can be expensive, ranging from hundreds to thousands of dollars.

While it may be tempting to delegate the task of credit repair to a credit repair business, it is important to understand what they can and cannot do – and to take action on your own before paying their fees.

If you believe the information in your credit file is inaccurate, credit repair companies may offer to dispute the information on your behalf with the credit reporting agencies. Credit repair firms usually charge a monthly fee for work completed in the previous month or a flat fee for each item removed from your credit reports.

That being said, it's important to remember that credit repair isn't a panacea – and in many instances, it crosses the line into unethical or even criminal practices by trying to delete information that has been correctly submitted to credit bureaus. Although these companies may attempt to refute any piece of negative information on your records, accurate information published by your lenders is unlikely to be removed.

And, once again, credit repair firms cannot do something that you cannot do for free on your own. As a result, it's a good idea to repair your reputation before paying a credit repair service to do it for you.

How to "Repair" Your Credit on Your Own

There is no easy remedy for your credit situation. Negative but correct information (such as late payments, charge-offs, or collection accounts) will stay on your credit report for seven to ten years. There are, however, steps you can take to begin building a more favorable credit history and gradually improve your credit scores. The better your personal credit status is, the better chance you will get a start-up loan or a loan to expand your business. Most investors and lenders want to be confident in the company's financial status in the company, particularly their credit status. The theory is that if you cannot manage your own finances, how can you handle those things? Also, if you are selling a product and your credit status is good, the product's manufacturer may be more likely to front you the product and allow you to pay for it after.

In fact, poor credit can easily cost you thousands of dollars a year in higher interest, larger fees, bigger premiums, extra loan points, and other hidden costs. Not only will that, but a single negative item on your credit report haunts you for years. On the other hand, having a high score will get you to credit when and where you need it. It increases your chances of landing better jobs, getting lower interest rates and fees. This is not only convenient but can save you thousands of dollars over some time.

For more reasons, a poor credit score can keep you from renewing a professional license or prevent you from getting utilities or cable connections in your new apartment/home. It can also prevent you from posting bail for yourself or someone else. There are literally hundreds of ways a poor credit score can negatively impact your life, and what is more, it can do so for years to come if you do not act on it.

In the course of this book, we will address several topics related to credit repair. We will look at how to improve our credit score and how to avoid being defrauded. All of the information in this book is the result of my 20 years of experience as a consultant. I hope that sharing my knowledge on the subject will be useful to you and allow you to improve your own and your family's financial situation.

Let's get started!

2. IS CREDIT REPAIR ETHICAL?

Beware, not all credit repair companies are ethical. Do not fall for scams that promise they can take a bad credit record and turn it around overnight. Or that guarantee they can "force" the credit bureaus to remove all negative (but accurate) information from your credit file immediately. It takes time and cooperation to improve your credit. Trust me when I tell you that a credit repair company cannot push around the large credit bureaus. Never mind order them to do things like immediately remove foreclosures or missed payments from the records of their clients. Inaccurate information can be easily fixed. However, removing accurate negative information takes a plan and is rarely done overnight. That usually requires filing official disputes and careful negotiations with your creditors.

Some credit repair companies not only misrepresent what they can do for you but also practice illegal or fraudulent ways of trying to improve your credit. Often, they will reorganize as a non-profit to get around state and federal laws that govern the industry. If you are desperate enough, you may be tempted to risk some of these illegal actions, but we would not recommend it. People have lost hundreds and, in some cases, thousands of dollars to credit repair scams.

Warning Signs When Choosing a Credit Repair Company

- They recommend that you do not contact credit bureaus directly.
- They do not disclose your legal rights or what you can do yourself.
- They want you to pay upfront based on their verbal promises before they do any work. They can only charge you after they have completed the services they contracted for.
- They suggest unethical or illegal actions such as making false statements on a loan application, misrepresenting your social security number, or obtaining an EIN number under false pretensions. The use of these tactics could constitute general fraud, civil fraud, mail fraud, wire fraud and get you into a lot of trouble.

The Disputing Process

The first thing you need to know is that all three credit reporting agencies have to contest the inaccurate information independently. The disputed appearance may be on all three credit reports or may not. Keep in mind that customers may not belong to all credit reporting agencies. This is why you will see that some of the investors are not on the others on one list.

Even though all three credit reporting agencies have the same information, this does not mean that if an item comes out of one credit report, it will come out of the others. No promise is provided what the outcome will be. That is why you have to refute any inaccurate information about each particular article.

They can use their appeal forms when disputing with credit reporting agencies, write your own message, or challenge the item online on their Website. If you decide to dispute by letter-writing, simply state the facts in a simple, concise or two sentences. If you choose to write a personalized message, you can also use the same answers as appropriate. Sample answers would be:

- This is not my account.

- This was not late as indicated.

- This was not charged off.

- This was paid off in full as agreed.

- This was not a collection account.

- This is not my bankruptcy as indicated.

- This is not my tax lien as indicated.

- This is not my judgment as indicated.

If you have found more than four entries on your credit report that you need to dispute, do not dispute everything in one letter. Whether you write a letter, fill out their form or answer via the Internet, break your disputes. You send or go back every 30 days to the credit reporting agency's website and challenge up to four more things. On submitting each address, expect to receive a revised credit report about 45 days after you send your letter or disagreement online. If your new credit report has not been issued before it is time to appeal the second time, go ahead and mail your second letter or challenge online instead.

Once all the grievance letters have been mailed or posted to their website, and all the revised credit reports have been received, check whether products have been omitted or incomplete. If you need to do the procedure again for the remaining items, space 120 days from your most recent update for another dispute.

What you should not do:

- Alter your identity or try to change it.

- The story is fictional.

- Check any information which is 100% correct.

What you should do:

• Read your emails, should you decide to send them to us? If a letter looks legitimate, credit reporting agencies will believe a credit repair service has written it, and they will not investigate the dispute.

- Use your original letterhead (if you do have one).
- Use the appeal form included with the credit report by the credit reporting agency, if you want.
- Provide some evidence suggesting the wrong entry is erroneous.
- Include the identification number for all communications listed on the credit report.

Spotting Possible Identity Theft

Checking your credit report could also spot potential identity theft. That is why you should inquire at least once a year or every six months for a copy of your credit report.

Things to look for would be:

- Names of accounts and figures that you do not know.
- You do not remember filling out loan applications.
- Addresses you did not live in.
- Poor bosses or tenants' inquiries you do not know.

Credit Rescoring

Rapid rescoring is an expedited way of fixing anomalies in the credit file of a customer. A fast rescore dispute process works through borrowers and mortgage brokers, a number of approved registry credit reporting companies, and credit reporting agencies.

If you are a creditor applying for a rescore on your credit report, you would need to provide detailed documents that would be sent to the collateral agencies that are working on your case. The cash registry is the system used by cash grantors. The data archive gathers the records from the three main credit reporting agencies and checks the consumer's initial information for a rescore. Once the verification is entered into the program of the repository, a new score will be produced.

The downside of a fast rescore is that you save money without having to contend individually with a credit reporting agency that may take longer than 30 days to complete an audit. If the sale of a house or lease depends on your credit score, and you are in a time crunch, the best solution is to easily restore.

First Step in Actually Repairing Your Credit

Write letters to the agencies with the correct but bad items you have encountered and your reasoning for which you think they should be taken off your credit report. When writing these letters and when making any type of contact with the people at the credit report agencies, the most important thing is to keep communication very polite and professional. The more pleasant and prepared you are, the more you increase the chances of helping you repair your credit. Sign and date your letters and try to write them by hand.

Contact with the Creditor

At this point, you have to write another letter, this time to the creditor. You can continue claiming that the negative information is wrong but be warned that they will not believe you if you do not provide solid proof to back up your claim. If you do not think you can muster up that proof to make a good case for re-establishing your good credit.

3. HOW TO ORDER A FREE CREDIT REPORT

Every single American citizen is entitled to one free copy of each of their credit reports every twelve months. The Fair Credit Reporting Act (FCRA) means that Transunion, Experian and Equifax are obligated to provide you with these details, but only if you ask for them. The FCRA promotes the privacy and accuracy of the information from these credit reporting agencies and is enforced by the Federal Trade Commission.

Assuming you visit the website, you will be sent to a form page where you will be required to include pertinent identifying information, including your date of birth, social security number, address and name. If you have moved within the previous two years, you will likely need to provide your previous address as well. Once you submit these details, you will then be taken to a page that will allow you to select the reports you wish to receive. You can choose to get all three at once or to get them one at a time, it doesn't matter as long as you haven't received them in the previous 12 months.

You will then be taken to a page that will further help to verify your identity. You will receive a list of questions about the terms of your loans, your current creditors, and the like that only you are likely to know.

There are pros and cons to pulling all three reports at once or waiting and spacing them out. If you decide to get your reports one at a time, then you can space them out throughout the year, one every four months, so that you will always be aware when something new affects your credit, negatively or positively. The downside is that if there is something negative on one of your credit reports and not the others, then you will have to wait a full year to find out about it.

On the other hand, pulling all three of your credit reports at the same time will allow you to pinpoint any issues right away, which means you can start working toward a solution for them as soon as possible. Additionally, this method will allow you to determine the differences between the various reports and any discrepancies that can be easily resolved, such as one of them not showing that you have finished paying off a loan. The downside is, of course, that if something happens to your credit in the next eleven months, you won't know about it until the time comes to pull all three again. To mitigate this fact, you can sign up with a credit monitoring service, which will monitor your credit for you in between the periods where you are eligible for a free copy of your various reports.

There are many ways to get your free credit report, but the one sponsored by the government is the best and most accurate way to go. This part you can do entirely online.

Start by visiting the website www.AnnualCreditReport.com. Then go to:

- Equifax   http://www.equifax.com/about-equifax/company-profile
- Experian http://www.experian.com/corporate/about-experian.html
- Transunion   https://www.transunion.com/about-us/about-transunion

You'll have to enter personal information and answer several security questions to verify your identity. Since you are looking at your own credit report, there will be no negative impact on your credit score. In addition, this is a highly secure government-run website. You can tell them whatever they want to know—they already know your underwear size anyway, if they believe that Snowden guy.

However you choose to get your copy, you will need that complete copy in order to start any disputes. Without it, you will be denied any attention by any of the credit bureaus and creditors.

Be aware of imposters

While AnnualCreditReport.com is the only legitimate way to pull your credit reports on a regular basis for free, that doesn't mean it is the only site out there offering this service. While these other sites might have offers for free services, they likely come with strings attached, at best, or are simply scams designed to steal your personal information, at worst. Especially be aware of sites whose URLs are misspellings of AnnualCreditReport.com as it is unlikely that they have anything remotely close to benign intentions in mind.

Likewise, the three major credit reporting agencies never contact individuals directly, which means if you receive a phone call or email from someone claiming to be with either Transunion, Experian or Equifax, then the safest choice is just to ignore it.

4. UNDERSTANDING FCRA AND SECTION 609

When you are going about trying to fix your credit, it can often feel as though the deck is stacked against you. However, the truth of the matter is that there are several laws that can help you to even the odds when it comes to dealing with both creditors and credit bureaus.

FCRA

The FCRA does more than just provide you with a free credit report each year; it also regulates the various credit reporting organizations and helps to ensure that the information they gather on you is both accurate and fair. This means that if you see inaccurate information on your credit report and report it to the relevant agency, they are legally required to look into the matter and resolve it, typically within 30 days. The same applies to agencies or organizations that generally add details to your credit report. Finally, suppose an organization that reviews your credit report decides to charge you more or declines to do business with you based on what they find in your report. In that case, they are legally obligated to let you know why and what report they found the negative information in.

While this won't help you with that particular lender, you will at least know where to go to clear up the issue if the information is inaccurate. Additionally, if you report inaccuracy and the credit reporting agency ignores your request, you can sue them to recover the damages or a minimum of $2,500. You may also win an additional amount based on punitive damages and legal fees, and any other associated costs. You must file legal proceedings within five years of when this occurs.

What Is Section 609? Is a 609 Dispute Letter Effective?

The first thing that we need to take a look at here when it comes to our credit scores is what Section 609 is really all about. Let's dive in now and see if we can learn a bit more about it.

This Act is going to limit the access that third parties can have to your file. You personally have to go through and provide your consent before someone can go through and look at your credit score, whether it is a potential employer or another institution providing you with funding.

They are not able to get in and just look at it. Keep in mind that if you do not agree for them to take a look at the information, it is going to likely result in you not getting the funding that you want because there are very few ways that the institution can fairly assess the risk that you pose to them in terms of creditworthiness.

There are several ways that a credit agency can go through and break or violate the FCRA, so this allows the consumer a way to protect themselves if that proves to be something that needs to happen.

Another thing to note about all of this is that the FCRA is going to be divided into sections. In particular, section 609 of the FCRA is going to deal with disclosure and is going to put all of the burdens of providing the right kind of documentation on the credit bureaus.

This may sound a little bit confusing, but it means that you may have debt or another negative item that is on your credit report, but there is a way to get around this without having to wait for years to get that to drop off your report or having to pay back a debt that you are not able to afford.

Keep in mind that this is not meant to be a method for you to take on a lot of debts that you can't afford and then just dump them. But on occasion, there could be a few that you can fight and get an instant boost to your credit score in the process.

You do not have to come up with a way of proving whether or not the item on the credit report is legitimate or not. Instead, that is up to the credit bureaus. And there are many cases where they are not able to do this. Whether they bought the debt and did not have the proper documentation, or there is something else that is wrong with it, the credit company may not be able to prove that you are the owner of it or that you owe on it at all. If this is the case, they have to remove the information from your credit report. When a bad debt is taken off, or even a collection is taken off, that does nothing but a lot of good for your overall score.

To take advantage of this law, the first thing you need to do is to send a physical letter to the billing inquiries address that the creditor provides. If they turn down your request, you can ask for all the documentation saying why they turned you down.

A subset of this law is known as the Hidden Gem Law; this means you can dispute any transaction made within 100 miles of your home or anywhere in your home state, which exceeds $50. If the debt collector breaks these rules or acts in other ways they are not allowed, then you can file a private lawsuit and be recouped costs, fees and damages. What's more, you don't even need to prove damages, and you will likely be awarded a minimum of $1,000.

Ways to Approach the Financial Institution

If the credit reporting agency is struggling to alter your report and you think the information is incomplete or wrong --you will want to take action. Below are a few suggestions that will assist you with your attempts.

Contact the Creditor Directly

Contact the lender, which supplied the advice and demand it to inform the credit. Request to Creditor composes your letter or to Eliminate. You can use inaccurate Information. You receive a letter from the lender and should be deleted from the credit history if you send a copy of the letter to the bureau that made the faulty report. If you contacted the Funding, it does not need to manage this dispute unless you supply it. But since you think you also demonstrate a foundation for the belief, and the dispute wasn't properly researched, should you increase your complaint, just like the president or CEO, the provider is very likely to reply. If the company cannot help you remove the inaccurate info, call the credit reporting agency.

Document another Dispute with the Credit Reporting Agency with More Information

If you have info that backs up your claim, it is possible to submit a fresh dispute. Make sure to provide info. Should you dispute the mistake without giving any info to the bureau, it will determine that your dispute is frivolous, so the bureau does not need to inquire into the issue.

Complaint about the Credit Reporting Agency

The CFPB attempt to have a response and will forward your complaint. If the CFPB believes another government agency will be able to assist you, it allows you to know and forward your complaint.

File a Complaint Concerning the Creditor

Suppose the lender supplied The erroneous or incomplete data fails to revise it or notify the credit reporting service of a correction (or even if it advises the credit reporting bureau of this alteration but reports the incorrect information again after). In that case, you might file a complaint with the Federal Trade Commission (FTC). Or, if the lender is a big institution, you might file a complaint. The CFPB manages Types of agencies, and that means a complaint can document. If you are not sure which agency to contact, begin with CFPB or even the FTC, which will forward your complaint. Normally, you won't be represented by these government agencies. However, they could send an inquiry, and they may take action when there are complaints or proof of wrongdoing.

Consider Adding an Explanatory Statement for Your Credit Report

You've got the right Statement for your credit score. As soon as you submit a statement regarding the dispute using a credit reporting agency, the agency must include your statement--or a list of it. It might limit your announcement.

In case the agency helps you in writing the excuse. There is not a term limit. Nonetheless, it is a fantastic idea to maintain the announcement shortly. In this way, the credit reporting agency is inclined to utilize your remark.

5. HOW TO PROCEED WITH THE LETTERS

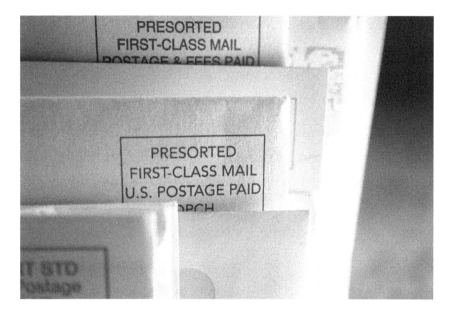

Before we get started here, we need to follow a few tips and rules to make sure that we are going to get the most out of the templates that we want to use.

These templates will help you compose and keep your dispute as organized as possible. When you pay attention to some of the details that are there, you will find that it is easier to come up with a convincing and effective letter.

There are a few different ways that we are able to make sure these letters get back to the right parties, and we are going to take a look at all of them below.

Emails

Our world seems to run online all the time, and finding ways to work on our credit scores and not have to waste a lot of time copying things or worrying about the paper trails can seem like a great idea. And in some cases, we may find that sending in our 609 letters through email is going to be the best situation for our needs.

You want the forms to end up in the right locations rather than getting sent to the wrong departments and not doing anything for you in the process. Most of the time, there will be listings for the various departments that you want to handle and work with for each credit agency, so take a look at those.

Again, when you are ready, you need to have as many details ready to go for this as possible. Just sending in a few lines about the process and thinking that will get things done is foolish. Write out a letter just like you would if you planned to send these by mail and use that as the main body of your email. Mention Section 609 and some of the disputes that you want to bring up.

In addition to this, you need to take some time adding in the other details. Attach some ways to prove your identity to the email, along with a copy of the credit report highlighted to show what is going on and what you would like to dispute. Add in any of the other documentation needed to help support your case and have it as clean and organized as possible to make sure the right people can find it and utilize this information to help you out.

Doing it All Online

Many of the credit agencies have made it easier to go through and work on some of these claims online. This helps you out because you will not need to go through and print it all off or worry about finding the paperwork or printing a bunch of things off. And if you are already on your credit report, your identification has been taken care of.

Since so many people are online these days, doing this right from the credit report is a simple and easy process to work with, and you will catch onto it fairly quickly. Do not take the easy way out with this. If you just click on the part that you think is wrong and submit a claim on it, this is not enough. There will not be any reference back to Section 609, and you will not be able to get them to necessarily follow the rules that come with Section 609.

This is where being detailed is going to be useful in the long run. When you do submit one of these claims online, make sure that you write a note with it to talk about Section 609, specifically the part of 609 that you want to reference in this dispute. You can usually attach other forms to document who you are and why you think these need to be dropped.

Treat this just like you would if you tried to mail the information to the credit agency. The more details that you are able to include in this, the better. This will help build up your case and make it harder for those items to stay on your credit report for a long time. Make sure to mention the 30-day time limit as well.

Telephone

A telephone is one method that you can use, but it is not usually the right one for this kind of process. For example, how easy is it going to be to show the credit agency what your driver's license looks like? You can repeat the number over if you would like, but this process is still a bit more laborious than some of the others and does not always work as well as we would hope it could.

However, this is definitely an option that we can use in order to reach the credit agencies, and for some people who are not sure of what their rights are or would rather talk directly to the individuals in charge about this issue, the telephone can be the right option. There is the possibility that the other side is going to have some questions for you, and they will at least want to go through and verify your identity to make sure they are ready to go. But the same rules apply here, and if you do not get a response within 30 days of that phone call, then the information should be erased.

Keep good records of the conversation, who you talked to during that time, what time and date it was, and so on. This will make it easier to get someone to respond to you and can help us to get this to work in our favor. Also, remember that you will need to repeat these phone calls to all three credit bureaus in order to get your information cleared on all of them.

Mail

Another option that you are able to work with is mail. This is usually a good method to use because it allows you a way to send in all of the information at once. Since you probably already have a physical copy of your SSN, driver's license, credit report and more, you can get copies of these made pretty quickly and then send them on with the Section 609 letter that you are working with. This method also allows us a way to go through and circle or highlight the parts of our credit report that we want to point out to the credit reporting agency.

This method is quick and efficient and will make sure that the information gets to the right party.

Certified Mail

For the most part, you are going to find that working with certified mail is going to be one of the best options that you can choose. This will ensure that the letter gets to the right place and can tell you for certain when the 30-day countdown is going to begin.

If you send this with regular mail, you have to make some guesses when the letter will arrive at the end address you want. And sometimes, you will be wrong. If there is a delay in the mailing and it gets there too late, then you may start your 30 days too early. On the other hand, if you assume it is going to take so many days and it takes less, you may wait around too long and miss your chance to take this loophole and use it to your advantage.

Certified mail is able to fix this issue. When the credit agency receives the letter, you will get a receipt about that exact date and even the time. This is going to make it so much easier for you to have exact times, and you can add these to your records. There is no more guessing along the way, and you can be sure that this particular loophole is going to work to your advantage.

Another benefit that comes with certified mail is that you make sure that it gets to its location. If you never get a receipt back or get something back that says the letter was rejected or not left at the right place, then you will know about this ahead of time. On the other hand, if it does get to its location, you will know this and have proof of it.

Sometimes things get lost. If the credit agency says that they did not receive the letter, you will have proof that you sent it and that someone within the business received it and signed for it. Whether the company lost it along the way or trying to be nefarious and not fix the issue for you, the certified mail will help you get it to all work for you.

When it comes to worrying about those 30 days and how it will affect you, have it all in writing and receipts to show what you have done and when it is going to be important.

6. CONTROLLING VARIOUS KINDS OF DEBT

Common Types of Debts

It depends on how you choose to see this. There are different kinds or types of debts. We will cut them into four groups to make this fun. Now, the first group.

1. Secured and Unsecured Loans.

Secured loans

Secured loans are the types of debts you get by offering something as surety if you don't pay that money up. For example, if you are buying a house, a car, or getting a big work machine, you may opt for a loan when you don't have enough funds to clear the bills yourself. Often, that is a lot of money, and your credit company wants to be sure you're paying it all without complications. So, you are asked to mortgage some of your valued assets in turn. They keep the documents until your payment is complete. If you don't pay up, there are a few legal actions to make, and they sell the assets. The norm is that you take this type of loan on significant assets.

Unsecured loans

Unsecured loans are the direct opposite of secured loans. You do not have to stake anything to access a loan like this. All you need is to indicate your interest, submit your essential documents, and the loan is yours. The type of loan you're asking for is what determines what you will be submitting. For example, your credit report may just be enough to get you another credit card. You may have to drop a little deposit plus your credit report when you're signing up for some utilities. All of these have a little or minimal risk for the user. Only that you can cover simple services with this type of loan, no more. Now, you can imagine which weighs higher on a credit score ranked by FICO.

2. Fixed and Revolving Payment Method

Fixed Payment Method

A lot of times, your credit company lays out clear terms, duration, and method of payment to you. When this happens, we say you have got a fixed payment method. Usually, fixed payment methods attract fixed interests too.

When you take part in a dealership deal, for example, you may be graced to get that money paid at a particular amount each month and a particular interest rate. Say, the car is worth a thousand USD. You are allowed to pay up in two years, with a total interest of 30%. That is pretty straightforward, right? That's just how fixed payment loans work. A mortgage is an example of fixed payment loans, so you might say they are pretty standard.

Revolving Payment Method

These types of loans are those that swing like unpredictable bells. There are no exact modalities on most items. You simply take the loans and pay as you can. For example, you can pay when you have the funds; there is no exact deadline for payments. You don't get a limit to interest rates too. Often, your utility, as well as your credit card, fall into this category. This is the exact reason you draw up a credit card, and you can use the credit card as much as you like each month. You don't have to pay up that money when the month ends. You can pay a little now, a lot more over the coming months. But as FICO had earlier advised, it makes perfect sense to draw up only 30% or less of your credit limits. Expectedly, your interest rate is determined by how promptly you clear off that debt.

3. Good and Bad Loans

No questions. This list can't be closed if this group isn't here.

The Good Loans

Classifying loans as good or bad does not exist in official records. Maybe if it did, nobody would ever be excited to try out the bad ones. In any case, a good loan is any loan drawn to invest in resources that may become useful and available over a long period, sometimes, forever. Some of them are:

Mortgage: If it is damning to size up your mortgage and you are planning to hand over the building, my sincere suggestion is that you keep pulling through, and you remain upbeat. This is one of the loans you can't ever regret taking. It is glaring to anyone that houses are assets that you don't use up any moment soon. A house may get into bad shape sometimes. That's normal. You are expected to keep it brimming with brightness naturally. If you do things right, you can't ever have to pay rent. You also have an asset you can risk to get huge loans to build your career. If things get worse, you can auction the house and restart your careers somewhere. However, you choose to see it, a loan drawn to get a house is a good one. Just be sure you can keep paying till the end before drawing the loan at all.

Student Loans: Well, you might hear someone say drawing student loans is insane. But if you look over the sayings, you'd have something different. You've got to get a good education, and you can't afford it at that moment. It makes perfect sense to tangle yourself in a loan, bag that degree, and pay back much more quickly. As you may fear, your first few years after school would be spent clearing your old debt. But you become free soon, and you'd have access to opportunities you may not have found without top training. From all viewpoints you see this, it is a win-win for all teams. So, I'd vote this as a good loan!

Business: Now, this is another perspective. If you are getting the loans to jack up your investments, you are settling for a good one too. It is undoubtedly a risk since the business may pick up and may not. But if you probably play your cards right, your business can boom, and that is the start of a goal you didn't see coming.

So, Bad Loans?

Auto loans: For a fact, you must be curious to know why auto loans should be tagged a bad debt, isn't it? I bet! Well, it is. Auto Loans, dealerships, and whatever kind of car loan you get into is a bad loan. This is because cars are not assets that can be used for a long while. If you sign a two or five-year loan deal, your car is already developing some sorts of problems. So, you'd have to spend on it, and at that same time, pay your auto loans. It would be a mess in a few years.

Credit Card Loans: Credit Card Loans are probably the worst you can take. They can't be used to get the important stuff. And either you take note or not, your debt is on the rise with every month you forgot to clear up.

Most Other loans: Most of the other types of loans fall into this category, especially those you draw from friends and family. They are often not precisely significant and should be avoided. Except, of course, they are critical to you, and you are sure there's some way you can quickly pay it all back.

How to Control Your Credit

Regardless of what credit types you have drawn, it is vital to monitor and control it all before it gets out of hand. Even if it's slipped a bit, the best option you've got is to find some way to monitor and control it. Hence, I'll be showing you some easy and practical ways in the next few lines. Here;

1.   Don't let things slip off: That's the first rule. Prevention is way better than cure. It stands to reason that if you can plan appropriately and watch out for sinking moments, you shouldn't have to fight to save your credit score fiercely. All you need is to do the math. Where are you heading to? What are your chances of hitting it big or terribly crashing? What would you have to do to avoid falling into a debt pit and struggling to pay up? Several things we might say. Your first job is to find those targets and set them working.

2.   Don't spend payments: Pending payments only increase your penalties. Whether for fixed and revolving debts. So, with the facts that you should avoid pending your payments. Clear them off the instant you are able to.

3.   Don't toy with revolving debts: Revolving debts are full of surprises. You would usually assume they are the littlest, so they can be paid after much bigger debts. In reality, your revolving debts (like your credit cards) cart

away more than your fixed debts. They tend to increase all the time, and there's a high potential for interest increase too, which doesn't happen in fixed credit cases. Hence, it washes that you should pay them up before considering some other debts at all. Don't delay others too!

If you do the math and your revolving debts are out, you will have a concrete idea of tackling the only other debts you have left. This itself is an acute style of controlling debts that you didn't notice. Now you know, cheers.

7. LITTLE KNOWN FACTS ABOUT CREDIT

Credit Cards Secrets Revealed

The first step when applying for a credit card is knowing the actual purpose why you are choosing to apply for a credit card in the first place. Some people find credit cards with cash rewards to be very attractive. At the same time, other people may want to apply for a credit card offering a 12 to the 18-month intro of 0% interest rate to make purchases without paying interest for a specific time and take advantage of balance transfers. There are many more reasons why consumers apply for credit cards, but it is important to know the ins and outs of the credit card so you can make well-informed decisions.

One of the most important things a consumer should know before applying for a credit card is their credit score. Consumers with excellent credit usually qualify for the best offers, but having average to poor credit often means a consumer will pay higher interest rates and possibly hefty annual fees.

Understanding Interest Rates

So, you recently applied for a credit card offering 0% for 6months, fast forward two weeks later, you checked your mail, and there it is, your brand-new credit card with a $5000 limit. You are thrilled because you were planning on using the credit card to book a trip to Cancun and pay off the card over the next five months. So you wasted no time booking your ticket and hotel room; you also purchased things you think are necessary for your trips, such as new clothes and shoes. Before long, your credit card balance jumped up to $4,500, but not to worry about now because you are planning on paying off your debt before the six-month intro zero percent grace period expires. Unfortunately, you were not able to pay off your credit card before the six-month interest grace period. To make matters worse, you were only making a minimum payment of approximately $105 every month. But six months later, your minimum payments were being applied to the interest and principal on your credit card balance instead of being applied to just the principal balance. Therefore, if you were to keep making the minimum payment of $105, it would have taken you 56 months to pay off the credit card. You would have also paid approximately $1,280 in interest payments.

<u>Annual Percentage Rate</u>

When you initially applied for a credit card, your annual percentage rate (APR) was 11.24%. However, what does this all mean to you? The APR is the annual cost of borrowing money from your credit card. The APR specifically applies to the interest rate that will be charged if your credit card balance is not paid in full on or before the due date.

<u>Types of APR</u>

There are usually several types of APR that apply to your credit card account. For example, there is an APR for purchases. There is an APR for a cash advance, balance transfers; an APR usually goes into effect when you make a late payment or violate any other terms of your credit card agreement.

Can My Credit Card Rate Increase?

Your credit card rate can increase if a promotional rate has expired, your credit card rate can increase when you don't follow your credit card terms when changes are made to a debt management plan and if your variable rate increases. What exactly is a debt management plan?

A debt management plan is an official agreement between a creditor and a debtor about a debt owed to the creditor by the debtor. The program is also designed to help the borrower pay off his or her outstanding debt faster. A debt management plan or debt relief plan is often a service a third-party company offers to someone who cannot afford to pay their debts on unsecured accounts. The third-party company (debt Relief Company) will collect the payment from the debtor and then distribute it to the creditor. A debtor often uses a debt relief company because it may help them evaluate their debt, help the debtor come up with a budget, establish a time frame to pay off their debt, and negotiate with creditors on their behalf.

A debtor usually enters into a debt management plan with a creditor when facing some financial hardship that makes it difficult for them to make even the minimum payments on their loan or credit card. The debt management plan will most likely include an agreement to allow the debtor to make an affordable payment to the creditor. The creditor will probably agree to dramatically reduce the interest rate on the debtor balance or outright eliminate the interest on the debtor balance.

Credit Bureaus

Credit bureaus are privately held, billion-dollar organizations whose primary reason for existing is to make cash; that is what revenue-driven organizations do, right? They keep data that lenders furnish them - whether accurate or inaccurate - about our credit association with them and sell it. This straightforward plan of action generates over $4 Billion per year!

One wellspring of income for them originates from selling the information on our credit reports to different lenders, managers, insurance agencies, credit card organizations - and whoever else you approve to see your credit information. In addition to the fact that they provide them with crude data, yet they likewise sell them various methods for examining the data to decide the risk of stretching out credit to us. In addition to trading our information to lenders, they likewise sell our information to us - credit scores, credit observing administrations, extortion security, wholesale fraud prevention - interestingly enough, this region has quickly gotten perhaps the greatest wellspring of income. Furthermore, those pre-endorsed offers in our letter drop each week; or garbage mail? That's right; they got our information from the credit bureaus as well. Organizations buy into assistance provided by the three credit bureaus that sell them a rundown of consumer credit information that fits a pre-decided criterion.

Presently, as opposed to prevalent thinking, credit bureaus don't have any contribution on whether you ought to be endorsed for a loan or not; that is absolutely based on the credit criteria of the lender you're working with. However, by utilizing the entirety of the information set on your credit report (personal information, payment history, and credit propensities) and FICO's technique for scoring that data, they tell them how creditworthy you are.

Origin and History of Credit Bureau

In recent decades, credit has gotten easier and easier to obtain. Credit cards, for example, were once given to the wealthier classes in the public eye and were utilized just occasionally. Toward the start of the twenty-first century, practically 50% of all Americans had in any event one broadly useful credit card (that is, a Visa, MasterCard, American Express, or Discover card). The ascent of credit as a typical method to buy necessities, extravagances, and everything in the middle of implies that credit bureaus process more information and are a more crucial part of the general economy than any other time in recent memory. Likewise, credit bureaus monitor and investigate the data from a regularly expanding number of loans for homes, cars, and other high-cost things.

Today, credit bureaus consistently accumulate information from creditors (banks; credit-card guarantors; mortgage organizations, which have practical experience in loaning cash to home buyers; and different businesses that stretch out credit to people and businesses) and amass it into files on singular consumers and businesses, while refreshing their current files. In addition to the data gathered from creditors, credit files may likewise contain one's business history, previous addresses, false names, bankruptcy filings, and removals. Information usually remains on a credit report for seven years before being evacuated.

The greater part of the nearby and provincial consumer credit bureaus in the United States is claimed by or are under agreement to one of the three essential consumer credit-reporting administrations referenced previously. Every one of these three organizations assembles and appropriates information separately, and credit scores and reports vary somewhat from bureau to bureau. Each organization keeps up around 200 million singular consumer credit files. Frequently a lender will utilize an average of the credit evaluations provided by the three unique bureaus when choosing whether to make a loan.

The basic business credit bureau in the United States is Dun and Bradstreet. D and B have credit files on more than 23 million associations in North America and more than 100 million businesses worldwide. In addition to giving creditors information important to decide a credit applicant's capabilities, credit bureaus make their data accessible for progressively questionable purposes. For example, standard mail advertisers regularly buy information from credit bureaus as they continued looking for potential clients. If you have ever gotten a letter revealing to you that you have been pre-endorsed for a particular credit card at a particular yearly percentage rate, it is valid; the credit-card organization definitely realizes your credit rating and has to be sure previously affirmed you for the predefined card.

Forthcoming managers and proprietors sometimes buy credit histories, as well.

What Credit Bureaus Do

Credit bureaus collect information from various sources in accordance with consumer information. The activity is done for various reasons and includes data from singular consumers. Included is the information concerning a people's charge payments and their getting. Utilized for evaluating creditworthiness, the information provides lenders with an outline of your accounts if a loan repayment is required. The interest rates charged on the loan are additionally worked out concerning the kind of credit score shown by your experience. Thusly, it is not a uniform procedure, and your credit report is the significant instrument that affects future loans.

Based on risk-based valuing, it pegs various risks on the various customers in this manner, deciding the cost you will acquire as a borrower. Done as credit rating, it is assistance provided to various interested parties in the public. Terrible credit histories are affected for the most part by settled court commitments that mark you for high-interest rates every year. Duty liens and bankruptcies, for example, shut you out of the conventional credit lines and may require a great deal of arrangement for any loan to be offered by the bank.

Bureaus collect and examine credit information, including financial data, personal information, and elective data.

Various sources give this, generally marked data furnishers. These have an exceptional association with the credit bureaus. An average gathering of data furnishers would comprise of creditors, lenders, utilities, and debt collection agencies. Any association that has had payment involvement in the consumer is qualified, including courts. Any data collected for this situation is provided to the credit bureaus for grouping. When it is accumulated, the data is placed into specific repositories and files claimed by the bureau. The information is made accessible to customers upon request. The idea of such information is important to lenders and managers.

The information is material in various conditions; credit evaluation and business thought are simply part of these. The consumer may likewise require the information to check their individual score, and the home proprietor may need to check their inhabitants' report before renting an apartment. Since borrowers saturate the market, the scores will, in general, be robotic. The straightforward examination would deal with this by giving the client a calculation for speedy appraisal. Checking your score once every other year should deal with errors in your report.

Individuals from the public are qualified for one free credit report from every one of the significant bureaus. Business reports, for example, Paydex, might be gotten to on request and are chargeable. Lawful expressions for the credit bureaus incorporate credit report agency, CRA in the US.

This is organized in the Fair Credit Report Act, FCTA. Other government rules associated with the assurance of the consumer incorporate the Fair and Accurate Credit Transaction Act, Fair Credit Billing Act and Regulation B. Statutory bodies have additionally been made for the regulation of the credit bureaus. The Fair Trade Commission serves as a controller for the consumer credit report agencies while the Office of the Comptroller of Currency fills in as a manager of all banks going about as furnishers.

<u>Transunion, Equifax and Experian</u>

Three Major Credit Bureaus

The popular credit bureaus significantly affect every consumer, but many people don't know these companies or how they work.

- Experian
- Equifax
- Trans Union

The ideal approach to manage your credit capably and assume responsibility for your financial circumstance is to be educated. This takes a brief period and exertion on your part, yet since your credit scores are so important to dealing with your accounts and setting aside cash, you have to know as much as you can regard the credit bureaus that formulate credit appraisals. To assist you with getting a running beginning on that strategy, some information on

Transunion, Experian and Equifax, the primary credit bureaus in the U.S.:

Transunion

Transunion has workplaces the nation over that manages various parts of credit: credit management, identity theft, and other credit issues; and types of credit customers, for example, personal, business, and press inquiries. If you discover errors on your Transunion credit report, you can call them at 800.916.8800 or visit their site to debate them. If that you believe that you're a casualty of identity theft, call them at 800.680.7289 at the earliest opportunity.

Experian

Like other credit bureaus, Experian provides a wide range of various administrations for people, businesses, and the media. Rather, they encourage guests to utilize online forms for questions, identity theft reports, and different issues.

Equifax

Based in Atlanta, GA, Equifax likewise has various departments to help people with various types of questions and concerns. Their website is set up to have people utilize online forms to address errors, report identity theft, and handle different concerns. In any case, if somebody believes that their identity has been taken, the individual in question can, however, call 888.397.3742 to report it to Equifax. If somebody detects a blunder on their Equifax credit report, that person must utilize the contact number on the report to question it. There is no number on the site to describe errors.

These are the 3 credit bureaus in the nation, and they each adopt an alternate strategy to enabling people to get in touch with them to pose inquiries or address any issues they might be encountering. Rather than reaching the credit bureaus legitimately, numerous people prefer to utilize a credit checking administration to assist them with dealing with their credit and stay over their funds. The credit bureaus all have comparative projects; however, most people prefer to utilize a free organization to assist them with these issues. That way, they get an impartial perspective on their credit score and a lot more devices to proactively manage and improve their credit ratings.

These companies have a great history in the financial industry. Also known as a credit reporting agency, it gathers financial information about consumers and combines it into a single report. Since these bureaus work independently, the credit report that a single bureau generates for an individual could be slightly different from another bureau's report. Although there are smaller credit bureaus, the top three serve a more significant share of the market.

The credit bureaus have a fascinating profit model. Lenders, banks, and many other companies share a lot of information about their clients with credit bureaus for free. The credit bureaus process this information and put it on sale, in the form of a credit report, to different parties that require insight into your financial history and more.

Thinking about just one number to represent your credit score is a little too simple. You actually have multiple credit scores, each calculated and maintained by a different company. Usually, these scores are very close to each other, but they almost always vary by at least a few points.

 The three bureaus are Equifax, Experian, and Transunion. We will get into the reason that the scores are different a little bit later, but it has to do with the way they collect information. Your score from any of these three companies will be called your FICO.../../Downloads/h - _ftn1 score (it may also be a BEACON score from Equifax). If it is called something different, it is just an estimate and is not the real deal. As we will find out later, that may be ok in some cases, but you should be aware of it.

 In addition to the three companies, each one actually keeps up to 7 different scores per person. We are just going to focus on what is called the classic or generic score for our purposes. So from here on out, the words "score" or "credit score" mean the classic or generic score. It is the most commonly used for most purposes (buying a house or getting a loan), and the other scores will follow it up or down for the most part. We aren't worried about two or three points here, we are looking for the biggest changes we can make with the least effort.

Dealing with Credit Bureaus

Today, where the economy is at its weak point, having good credit is a necessary tool. This is because it allows you to obtain house loans, car loans, credit cards, and other convenient financial services and instruments. You may be able to live without having good credit.

You can discern the credit bureau that holds your file by looking at any rejection letter you received from a recent credit application.

If you are dealing with the credit bureau that handles your file, keep in mind that it belongs in the business of collecting and selling information. As such, you should not provide them with any detail, which is not necessarily legal.

When you already have your credit report, make sure to check for any errors or discrepancies. If you find anything that is questionable in your report, you can send the credit bureau a written request to investigate In general, the credit bureau has the burden of documenting anything that is included in your credit report. If the credit bureau fails to investigate the error or neglects your request for an investigation within 30 days, the error should be removed.

You need to educate yourself about the legal obligations of credit bureaus to have a successful credit repair process. Before dealing with them, make sure you know all the legal aspects so you would not end up paying for something that should not be charged with a fee. Remember, credit bureaus are also businesses and that they own many credit repair companies.

Making the Best of Credit Bureaus

It is a little annoying to learn that all three credit bureaus have sensitive financial data. However, there's no method to prevent lenders and collection entities from sharing your information with the above companies.

You can limit any possible problems associated with the credit bureaus by evaluating your credit reports annually and acting immediately if you notice some errors. It is also good to monitor your credit cards and other open credit products to ensure that no one misuses the accounts. If you have a card that you don't often use, sign up for alerts on that card to get notified if any transactions happen and regularly review statements for your active cards. Next, if you notice any signs of fraud or theft, you can choose to place a credit freeze with the three credit bureaus and be diligent in tracking the activity of your credit card in the future.

How the Bureaus Get Their Information

To learn how the score is calculated, we need to learn about all the different inputs of your score, aka where the bureaus get their info. You may have many factors that report information to the credit bureaus or none.

Credit cards are called revolving accounts or revolving debt by the credit bureaus. Each monthly payment and balance is reported, as well as any late payments. This means that any cards that have your name on them will also report to all the bureaus. This includes cards that belong to a spouse or parent. If you're an authorized user on the account, it gets reported on your credit no matter what. Many people have their credit ruined by a spouse or parent going into bankruptcy or not paying their credit card bills. If your name is on any credit cards that belong to people that may not pay their bills, ask them to take your name off immediately!

Installment loans also report information to the credit bureaus. If you went down to your local Sears and financed a washer/dryer set by putting up a down payment, that is an installment loan. The details of these loans are all reported; the total balance, as well as the timeliness and amounts of your monthly payments.

If you have mortgages or student loans, that information does get reported. Total amounts due, total paid so far, and the status of monthly payments is all reported. This information is all kept track of and organized in their databases.

8. HOW TO OVERCOME CREDIT CARD DEBT

What is a Credit Card Debt?

When you incur a credit card debt, you actually keep borrowing money every month, which is also known as revolving debt. But it is only good until you can repay them, but when you can't, the debt keeps accumulating. When compared to the loan accounts, you can actually keep using your credit card accounts for an indefinite time. There is nothing that the company can seize in simpler terms, like a house or a card, even when you have failed to repay them. But yes, if you cannot repay the money you borrowed from the credit card, it will affect your credit score drastically.

How Is Credit Card Debt Accumulated?

When you get a credit card, you will see that there will be a due date within which you have to clear the entire balance you have accumulated on your credit card, and if you fail to do so, you will be accumulating debt. There is a term called APR or Annual Percentage Rate, and this is a rate of interest charged on your debt when it keeps accumulating one month after the other. The APR that you will be charged may not be the same as someone else's, and this is because it keeps differing with your credit history, the bank issuer, and the type of card you have.

The benchmark fed funds rate of the Federal Reserve and the prime rate of the credit card interests is somewhat tied, and that is the average value. The credit card debt will increase or decrease concerning any changes in the target rate made by the Fed.

Now, I want to give you an even clearer picture of how this debt accumulates. There is a minimum payment for starters that you will have to pay every month whenever you use your credit card to make purchases. This payment is calculated based on a certain percentage (with some additional interest charges) of your balance. If you pay this amount in full, then well and good, but if you don't, then you will be liable to interest. So, the interest will increase if you pay even lesser. This is because the nature of credit card interests is compounding, so the interest keeps accruing. Thus, if you take a longer time to clear off the debts, then you will owe a huge amount of money to the company, which is much more than what you actually owed before.

What Happens After 7 Years?

This is basically a time limit until which a record is shown in a credit report. But certain other negative issues will stay in your credit report even after seven years, for example, certain judgments, unpaid tax liens, and bankruptcy.

But you also have to keep in mind that if any debt is unpaid, then it is not exactly going to vanish even after seven years. Even if the credit report does not list it, you will still owe that money to the lender.

Several other legal ways can be implemented by lenders, creditors, and debt collectors to collect the debt that you haven't paid. Some of these methods include a court giving permission to garnish your wages, sending letters, calling you, and so on. One thing that you benefit from because of this seven- years rule is that when the debt is no longer visible on your credit report, it cannot affect your credit score. Thus, you can actually have a better chance of gaining back a good score. Another thing to keep in mind is that this seven-year term is only for the negative information on your report and not the position information because they will stay on the report forever. You should keep an eye out after the seven-year mark as to whether the credit bureaus have removed that information or not. They usually do it automatically, but if they don't, you will have to raise a dispute.

Many people have this question of what happens to their debt if they accidentally die. Well, in that case, it will be your estate that will be used to pay the debt off. Remember that the debt will not be shoved in someone else's hand in your family because whatever money you owe, it is your debt and not anyone else's. And so whatever you had, like your accounts and assets, will then be used for clearing the debt. And after that, if anything remains from your assets, your heir will receive it.

How to Eliminate Credit Card Debt?

Start Eliminating High-Interest Debts First

When you are trying to eliminate your credit card debt, the biggest obstacle that will stand in your way is carrying a very high rate of interest. Sometimes, the interest rate can even be in double- digits, sometimes as high as 22%. In that case, paying it off can be a really difficult task. But the reason why I am asking you to start eliminating them first because when you have cleared these debts, you will have a greater amount of money left in your hand at the end of each month.

Another thing that you could do, but only if you have enough credit available, is to apply for a new credit card. But this should be a zero-interest one. Once you get it, transfer the balance to eliminate the high-interest debt. Yes, I know that some of you might be thinking that it is not a sensible thing to do to apply for another credit card, and that is why I will be asking you to get it only if you think you have enough self-restraint not to go buy a bunch of stuff that you don't need.

Keep Making Small Payments

Quite contrary to the technique I mentioned above is another technique which is called the snowflake technique. With this process, you will be making small payments towards your debt every time you get some extra cash in hand. Whatever payment you are making, it does not matter as long as you keep paying.

You can pay $10, or you can pay $20, but at the end of the year, you will find that you have reduced about $1000 simply by paying such small amounts almost every day, even if you are paying $2 on any particular day.

People often ignore this method, thinking that it will be only small amounts, but you should not make the mistake of overlooking these small amounts as they have quite the power in them. When you are making these small payments, it would feel as if they are not even leaving any dent, but they will sum up and cause a considerable effect on your debt with time.

Preventive Measures to Avoid Credit Card Debt

Have an Emergency Fund

Think about a situation when you have encountered a problem that requires you to spend a lot of money, for example, a car repair or job loss or medical emergencies.

But why arrive at such a situation when you can build an emergency fund that will cover at least six months' expenses. A fund of this size will help you to figure out any small expenses that crop up overnight. Take your time to build your emergency fund to not have to rely on debt ever.

Buy Only What You Can Afford

When you have a credit card in hand, it can get really tempting, and you start buying whatever you think you want. If not, then don't buy it now. Make a goal to save the money required for purchasing that item instead of buying it on credit.

Don't Transfer Balance If Not Necessary

Some people have this habit of clearing their balance with a higher credit card, but such repeated balance transferring can actually backfire on you. When you keep transferring balanced without keeping track of your activities, you might end up with an ever-increasing balance, and you will also have to clear the fee requires for all those transfers.

Try Not Taking out a Cash Advance

Sometimes, you may be in the moment, and you were not thinking clearly so, you decide to take a cash advance. Moreover, you will have to realize that you are getting into credit card debt if you have started making cash advances. The moment you see it happening, you will have to start working on that emergency fund and also tweak your budget.

Lastly, I would like to say that no matter how many measures you take, try avoiding increasing your credit cards unnecessarily. The more the number of credit cards, the more you will have to stop yourself from overspending.

9. THE CREDIT BUREAUS: GENERAL NOTIONS

Credit bureaus are privately held, billion-dollar organizations whose primary reason for existing is to make cash; that is what revenue-driven organizations do, right? They keep data that lenders furnish them - whether accurate or inaccurate - about our credit association with them and sell it. This straightforward plan of action generates over $4 Billion per year!

One wellspring of income for them originates from selling the information on our credit reports to different lenders, managers, insurance agencies, credit card organizations - and whoever else you approve to see your credit information. In addition to the fact that they provide them with crude data, yet they likewise sell them various methods for examining the data to decide the risk of stretching out credit to us. In addition to trading our information to lenders, they likewise sell our information to us - credit scores, credit observing administrations, extortion security, wholesale fraud prevention - interestingly enough, this region has quickly gotten perhaps the greatest wellspring of income. Furthermore, those pre-endorsed offers in our letter drop each week; or garbage mail? That's right; they got our information from the credit bureaus as well. Organizations buy into assistance provided by the three credit bureaus that sell them a rundown of consumer credit information that fits a pre-decided criterion.

Presently, as opposed to prevalent thinking, credit bureaus don't have any contribution on whether you ought to be endorsed for a loan or not; that is absolutely based on the credit criteria of the lender you're working with. However, by utilizing the entirety of the information set on your credit report (personal information, payment history, and credit propensities) and FICO's technique for scoring that data, they tell them how creditworthy you are.

Origin And History Of Credit Bureau

In recent decades, credit has gotten easier and easier to obtain. Credit cards, for example, were once given to the wealthier classes in the public eye and were utilized just occasionally. Toward the start of the twenty-first century, practically 50% of all Americans had in any event one broadly useful credit card (that is, a Visa, MasterCard, American Express, or Discover card). The ascent of credit as a typical method to buy necessities, extravagances, and everything in the middle of implies that credit bureaus process more information and are a more crucial part of the general economy than any other time in recent memory. Likewise, credit bureaus monitor and investigate the data from a regularly expanding number of loans for homes, cars, and other high-cost things.

Today, credit bureaus consistently accumulate information from creditors (banks; credit-card guarantors; mortgage organizations, which have practical experience in loaning cash to home buyers; and different businesses that stretch out credit to people and businesses) and amass it into files on singular consumers and businesses, while refreshing their current files. In addition to the data gathered from creditors, credit files may likewise contain one's business history, previous addresses, false names, bankruptcy filings, and removals. Information usually remains on a credit report for seven years before being evacuated.

The greater part of the nearby and provincial consumer credit bureaus in the United States is claimed by or are under agreement to one of the three essential consumer credit-reporting administrations referenced previously. Every one of these three organizations assembles and appropriates information separately, and credit scores and reports vary somewhat from bureau to bureau. Each organization keeps up around 200 million singular consumer credit files. Frequently a lender will utilize an average of the credit evaluations provided by the three unique bureaus when choosing whether to make a loan.

The basic business credit bureau in the United States is Dun and Bradstreet. D and B have credit files on more than 23 million associations in North America and more than 100 million businesses worldwide. In addition to giving creditors information important to decide a credit applicant's capabilities, credit bureaus make their data accessible for progressively questionable purposes. For example, standard mail advertisers regularly buy information from credit bureaus as they continued looking for potential clients. If that you have ever gotten a letter revealing to you that you have been pre-endorsed for a particular credit card at a particular yearly percentage rate, it is valid; the credit-card organization definitely realizes your credit rating and has to be sure previously affirmed you for the predefined card. Forthcoming managers and proprietors sometimes buy credit histories, as well.

What Credit Bureaus Do

Credit bureaus collect information from various sources following consumer information. The activity is done for various reasons and includes data from singular consumers. Included is the information concerning a people's charge payments and their getting. Utilized for evaluating creditworthiness, the information provides lenders with an outline of your accounts if a loan repayment is required. The interest rates charged on loan are additionally worked out concerning your experience's kind of credit score. Thusly, it is not a uniform procedure, and your credit report is the significant instrument that affects future loans.

Based on risk-based valuing, it pegs various risks on the various customers in this manner, deciding the cost you will acquire as a borrower. Done as credit rating, it is assistance provided to various interested parties in the public. Terrible credit histories are affected for the most part by settled court commitments that mark you for high-interest rates every year. Duty liens and bankruptcies, for example, shut you out of the conventional credit lines and may require a great deal of arrangement for any loan to be offered by the bank.

Bureaus collect and examine credit information, including financial data, personal information, and elective data. Various sources give this, generally marked data furnishers. These have an exceptional association with the credit bureaus. An average gathering of data furnishers would comprise of creditors, lenders, utilities, and debt collection agencies. Any association that has had payment involvement in the consumer is qualified including courts. Any data collected for this situation is provided to the credit bureaus for grouping. When it is accumulated, the data is placed into specific repositories and files claimed by the bureau. The information is made accessible to customers upon request. The idea of such information is important to lenders and managers.

The information is material in various conditions; credit evaluation and business thought are simply part of these. The consumer may likewise require the information to check their score, and the home proprietor may need to check their inhabitants' report before renting an apartment. Since borrowers saturate the market, the scores will, in general, be robotic. The straightforward examination would deal with this by giving the client a calculation for speedy appraisal. Checking your score once every other year should deal with errors in your report.

Individuals from the public are qualified for one free credit report from every one of the significant bureaus. Business reports, for example, Paydex might be gotten to on request and are chargeable. Lawful expressions for the credit bureaus incorporate credit report agency, CRA in the US. This is organized in the Fair Credit Report Act, FCTA. Other government rules associated with the assurance of the consumer incorporate Fair and Accurate Credit Transaction Act, Fair Credit Billing Act and Regulation B. Statutory bodies have additionally been made for the regulation of the credit bureaus. The Fair Trade Commission serves as a controller for the consumer credit report agencies while the Office of the Comptroller of Currency fills in as a manager of all banks going about as furnishers.

Credit Inquiries

Next is Credit Inquiries. As Latoya Irby, a credit analyst chooses to put it; Credit Inquiries is a general term that covers all investigations and requests for your credit report. As you now understand, credit companies want you to have a credit report before accessing their services; as such, you are bound to create a credit report before you get real loans. But the credit companies don't just want you to set the records. They want to explore it.

Practically, this means that each time you call for loans in a credit company, you are bound to permit them to request your credit report from a credit bureau. They usually do, and the detail of each inquiry is inserted in the next credit report. For example, if A/B Company had requested your report at some point, and KYC Company had also requested, JJC Company will find these companies in your credit report when you apply for another credit with them. That way, they can tell the other people you have contacted, how 'desperate' you have been finding some credit, and how unsuccessful you have been.

10.   RIGHT MINDSET FOR CREDIT MANAGEMENT

Financial problems can be and usually are overwhelming. To make these situations worse, most people do not even know where to begin to solve these financial dilemmas.

Basic consumer debt will chain you into slavery, and you could possibly spend your life held down by your own obligations to repay these loans.

Since your ability to repay a loan has been affected, either by the inability to pay or a series of misunderstandings, other lenders will become skeptical when it comes to granting you new credit.

Useful Tips & Tricks

What type of credit should you get?

The most used types of credit are secured and signature credits. For smaller loans, there's no need for that, as no institution would like to end up with a store of household items, so they lend you money or issue a credit card in your name simply based on the strength of your credit so far.

You can take advantage of budgeting and other techniques, such as debt consolidation, debt settlement, credit counseling, and bankruptcy procedures. You just have to choose the best strategy that will work for you. When choosing from the various options, you have to consider your debt level, discipline, and future plans.

Using consolidation or settlement strategies to pay down debts

Debt consolidation is another strategy that can be used to manage your debts. It involves combining two or more debts at a lower interest rate than you are currently at.

But it is worth doing your research and making some phone calls to see if there is a company that is willing to work with you. If you can lower your monthly bill to a manageable level at a reasonable interest rate, that can make all the difference in handling your debt. It is just that consolidation and settlement options rose in popularity during the recent financial crisis making it appear in more articles and news pieces than ever before.

Negotiate with Credit Companies

So you are able to take the collection letter they send you or a past due notice that has been sent to you and discuss it with them. In many cases, they will take a lower amount than what is on the bill just so that they can guarantee they will get something

If you talk to the collection agency and agree to take a lesser amount, you will have to send that payment in full. Make sure that when you send them the check, you write out the words 'paid in full' on the check. Make a copy of the check for your own records as well. Once they cash that check, your account is legally considered to be paid in full, and they are no longer able to come after you for more money.

Cut the Credit Cards

Choose a card that will work anywhere, such as a major credit card company.

The best thing to do is make one to two small purchases on your credit card every few months. Try to space out using different cards so that none of them get taken, but you do not owe very much money each month.

Talking to Creditors

Tell them the reason why you are having a difficult time paying the debts. Most companies will negotiate a modified payment plan, so monthly payments become more manageable. If you wait for the accounts to go into default, it can most likely affect your credit score negatively, which is what we are looking to avoid. Once in default, the collector will start calling.

Credit Counseling

Credit counseling is a service offered by some organizations to borrowers seeking advice on managing their finances. It usually includes budgeting, workshops, and educational resources. A counselor must receive training and certification in budgeting, money and debt management, and consumer credit.

Debt Management Plan

The credit counselor negotiates with the creditors and drafts a payment schedule. Creditors may be amenable to waive some fees or reduce interest rates. Usually, a debt management plan takes about 4 years to be completed, depending on your amount of debt.

Debt Settlement Program

A debt settlement program can be risky, so you have to consider some factors before taking advantage of it. Many of these programs require that you deposit money on an account for at least 3 years before the debt settlement company can settle your debts.

Another aspect to consider is that some creditors will not negotiate for a debt settlement; therefore, the debt settlement company may not be able to pay some of your debts. In addition, some of these debt settlement companies pay off smaller debts first, leaving the large debts to continue growing.

The debt settlement company will suggest that you stop paying your creditors. This decision will result in a significant drop in your credit score. The debts will also incur fees and penalties for nonpayment.

Goodwill Letters

Goodwill letters are not a guaranteed method of removing negative information from your credit report but are still worth a try in some situations. If you have a good history with the company, they are more effective, have had a technical error delayed your payment, or if your auto pay did not go through. You can sometimes even convince a credit company to forgive a late payment if you simply forgot to pay.

Try to contact your credit agency by phone to negotiate and explain your situation before sending a goodwill letter. This tactic might be all that you need to do to remove the record of the late payment. The sooner you contact, the better as well. If you notice that you have a late payment, calling right away could stop it from being reported at all.

To write a goodwill letter you should:

- Use courteous language that reflects your remorse for the late payment and thank the company for their service.
- Include reasons you need to have the record removed, such as qualifying for a home or auto loan or insurance.
- Accept that you were at fault for the late payment.
- Explain what caused the payment to be made late.
- To write a goodwill letter, you should not:
- Be forceful, rude, or flippant about the situation.

Goodwill Letter Template

Date

Your Name

Your Address

Your City, State, Zip Code

Name of Credit Company

Address

City, State, Zip Code

Re: Account Number

Dear Sir or Madame,

Thank you [company's name] for continued service. I am writing in regard to an urgent request concerning a tradeline on my credit reports that I would like to have reconsidered. I have taken pride in making my payments on time and in full since I received [name of credit line/card] on [date that you received the credit].

Unfortunately, I was unable to pay on time [date of missed payment(s)] due to [detailed and personal reason for not being able to pay on time. You might want to include several sentences using as much information as possible to plead your case.]

[Follow up your reason for not paying on time with a concession of guilt such as:] I have come to see that despite [reason listed above], I should have been better prepared/more responsible with my finances to ensure the payment was on time. I have worked on [some type of learning or way of improving your situation] in order to prevent this situation from happening again.

I am in need of/about to apply for [new credit line such as a home loan] and it has come to my attention that the notation on my credit report of [credit company's] late payment may prevent me from qualifying or receiving the best interest rates. Due to the fact that this notation is not a reflection of my status with [Credit Company], I am requesting that you please give me another chance at a positive credit rating by revising my trade lines.

If you need any additional documentation or information from me in order to reach a positive outcome, please feel free to contact me.

Thank you again for your time,

Sincerely yours,

Your Name / Signature

11. BEST HABITS TO ACHIEVE YOUR FINANCIAL FREEDOM

When it comes to financial freedom, there are dozens of habits and tips that people provide to help you reach your financial freedom. It is important to note that because financial freedom can vary depending on the person's definition, some of the tips and habits might work for you while others may not. You need to find the ones that work best for you, not the ones that other people say are the best.

Make a Budget

Making and keeping a budget is one of the first steps everyone should take while heading towards financial freedom. Even though you might find yourself changing your budget now and then, as you will add or delete bills or receive a different income, you always want to follow it. Not only will this help you in reaching your financial freedom, but continuing to follow your budget will also protect your financial freedom.

Furthermore, creating a monthly budget can make sure that all your bills are being paid and you know exactly where your money is going. This will help you know where you can decrease your spending, which will allow you to save more.

Set Up Automatic Savings Account

If you work for an organization that automatically places a certain percentage of your check into a savings account, take advantage of this. It gives you the idea that you never had the money to begin with, which means you don't plan for it, and you won't find yourself taking the money out of savings unless you need it for an emergency. Furthermore, you can set up a separate savings account where this money will go. You can make it, so you rarely see this account, however, you want to make sure that your money is deposited and everything looks right on your account. But, the point of this account if you do not touch it, even if you have an emergency. Instead, you will set up a different account on an emergency basis.

The other idea to this is you pay yourself first. This is often something that people don't think about because they are more worried about paying off their debt.

Keep Your Credit in Mind without Obsessing Over It

One factor to remember is that your credit score is typically only updated every so often. Therefore, you can decide to set time aside every quarter to check on your credit report. When you do this, you not only want to check your score, but you also want to check what the credit bureaus are reporting. Just like you want to make sure everything is correct on your bank account, you want to do the same thing for your credit report.

It Is Fine to Live Below Your Means

One of the biggest factors of financial freedom and maintaining it is you can make your bills and comfortably live throughout the month. In order to do this, you need to make sure that the money coming into your home is more than the money going out. In other words, you want to live below your means.

This is often difficult for a lot of people because they want to have what other people have. They want to have the newer vehicles, the bigger boat, the newest grill, or anything else. People like to have what their friends and neighbors have. However, people don't think about one factor because their friends and neighbors probably don't have financial freedom. Therefore, you want to take a moment to think about what is more important for you. Would you rather be in debt like your friends, or would you rather have financial freedom?

Speak With a Financial Advisor

Sometimes the best step we can take when we are working towards financial freedom is to talk with a financial advisor. They can often give up information, help us with a budget, make sure that we get the most out of our income, and tell us where we might be spending more money than we should. Furthermore, they can help you figure out what the best investments are, which are always helpful when looking at financial freedom. At the same time, they can help you plan for your retirement, which is one of the biggest ways you will remain financially free.

Completely Pay Off Your Credit Cards

If you are high-interest credit cards, which is often the case, you want to make sure that you pay these off every month. Therefore, your credit card spending should become part of your budget. What this means is you don't want to use your credit card for whatever you feel like. Instead, you want to create a list of when you can and when you can't use your credit card. For example, you might agree that it is fine in emergencies or during Christmas shopping. You might also feel that you can use it during tips because it has trip insurance. Whatever you decide, you want to make sure you follow.

Track Your Spending

Along with making sure you follow your budget, you also want to track your spending. There are several reasons for this. First, it will help you make sure that your budget is on track. We often forget about automatic bills paid monthly or don't realize how much we really spend every month. These factors can make our budget off, which can cause an obstacle when you are working to reaching and keeping your financial freedom.

Fortunately, there are a lot of apps that you can download. Many of them are free, which will allow you to easily track your spending. Some of these apps include Mint or Personal Capital. These apps typically give you all the information you need and will automatically tell you how much you are spending and how much income you still hold at the end of the month. Most of these apps will also give you charts to help you see your spending habits differently.

Continue Your Education

Another way to stay on top of your financial freedom is to become educated regarding your budget, spending, taxes, and anything else to do with your finances. You can simply do your own research or take online classes, some of which you will find are low-cost to free. You can also look into webinars that people hold.

You can also help yourself when it comes to investing in the stock market or anything else. There are always several classes you can take online, which only have a few sessions or ways to learn when you have the time. In fact, if you want to invest but don't know what to do or where to begin, one of your best options is to take a class.

Make Sure to Keep Your Mindset

This is a mindset that you will want to continue to have while you are living financially free. With this mindset, you will not only feel grateful for where you are in life, but you will also remember where you once were. This will help you work towards protecting your financial freedom instead of falling back into credit card debt.

Of course, you can adjust your mindset the way you want to once you reach financial freedom. However, you will want to make sure that you keep your mindset positive. After all, a positive mindset makes you believe that you can accomplish anything.

Make Sure You Write Down What Financial Freedom Means to You

Financial freedom can mean something different to you than it means to someone else. Because of this, you have to think about what it truly means to you. Whatever you feel it means, it is important to write this down. This will allow you to turn back to what financial freedom means to you when you find yourself struggling and feeling like you can't gain your financial freedom.

Think of what you want to accomplish on your road to financial freedom. You can also think about what you want to do after you have reached financial freedom. Give yourself goals to work towards, as this will help you stay on track better.

12.   RE-ESTABLISHING YOUR CREDIT

The road to re-establishing your credit can be a bumpy one, especially if you have to start over from scratch.

Whatever your goals are, once your credit report has gotten the boost needed, the efforts to reestablish your credit should begin with you. While you may have big dreams, you need to recover slowly. You don't want to make a misstep and end up falling back down the rabbit hole again.

Often, after having a rough bout with credit, the tendency is to swear off credit for good. The vow to go strictly cash can be strong after surviving a difficult time with creditors and bill collectors. In fact, it could make it even more difficult for you later on. You've learned your lesson about bad credit, but you are smarter now, and you know that credit itself is not the bad guy, it's how you use it.

You now have a credit goal, and you know what to do with it. You know how much credit you can charge and still keep your score high, and you know the importance of making timely payments. You have all the tools you need in your arsenal to start your rebuilding campaign.

Step 1: Know How Much Credit You Need

This will give you a general idea of just how much credit you should have.

For this, you need to determine your debt to income ratio. When you are ready to apply for new credit, lenders will look at this percentage to decide on giving you credit.

The formula for this is simple. Take you're total from your list of financial obligations and divide it by your gross monthly income. It will give you the percentage of credit you should have in your arsenal. For example, if your monthly income is $1500.00 and your total monthly expenses are $800, the formula should look like this.

$800/1500 = 53\%$

The higher this percentage is, the less likely a creditor will be willing to issue you knew credit, even with a good score.

Step 2: Start Small

You may have big dreams but keep them within realistic boundaries. Remember, you're trying to recover from credit illness. If you had been physically ill to the point where you needed hospitalization, you wouldn't come home from the hospital and automatically resume your same routine. You will build up your strength a little at a time until you were back to the same physical condition you were before.

You should view rebuilding your credit in the same way. Don't look to establish an unsecured bank credit card fresh out of the gate. These are probably the most difficult to get.

When filling out your application, here are a few things to keep in mind to make the process go smoother, and the results will lean more in your favor.

Do not put in more than three applications for credit in a single month. More than that, and your score will drop.

Don't add anything to your application that won't benefit you in some way. Some businesses will allow you to make purchases without established credit but will only report to the credit bureau once you've paid it off. Only put these on your application if you've made regular payments, and you know it will boost your score.

Only apply to those that will raise your overall credit score.

As the months go by and you are making regular payments, you can begin to increase your purchase amounts little by little. Your creditor will notice that you are spending wisely and will likely drop the need for security behind the card you have and perhaps even increase your limit. Remember, they make their money by charging interest, so the more money you borrow, the more they can earn. Still, you don't have credit to support them, so maintain self-control and stay within your limits, and your score will naturally increase.

Step 3: Protect What You Have

No matter how much or how little credit you have, never take it for granted. Make sure that you follow the rules, and your credit should stay in good condition.

With revolving credit (credit cards), avoid using them too often. Only charge as much as you can reasonably pay off within a given month. No doubt, you will continue to hit rough patches here and there; even people with good credit need to be prepared. With credit that you use infrequently, make it a habit of making a small purchase from time to time so that the account does not become inactive. Then pay off the total balance immediately when you do.

Establish a rapport with your creditors. That way, if you end up paying late one month, you have a friend you can call that can help you to recover quickly. Missing a payment or paying late can be the death knell for a newly recovered credit score; the more friends you have in your corner, the more likely you will come out on top when that happens.

Step 4. Use automation when you can.

There are several ways to do this.

It is pretty easy to make up automatic payment arrangements through any of these plans but arranging it directly with your creditor is probably the fastest and simplest way to do it.

This decision works best for those who have a regular monthly income that they can be sure will be in their bank at the right time. At the end of the day, the main goal is to never be late or miss a payment so you can avoid falling behind and running into a lot more problems than you bargained for.

You're in It for the Long Haul

When you're under a lot of pressure from collection agencies and creditors, it is easy to think that repairing credit and getting back on track is an emergency, but your credit will be with you for the long term. You won't be able to address some things immediately, and you will have to wait it out.

Don't rush the process, but instead, take your time, be methodical in your approach, and the chances of your clearing up your good name are quite good.

Focus on the future, not the immediate present, and you will be driven to make sure that every step you take will be sustainable, and you will be able to establish and maintain your new credit score for years to come.

13.   THE THREE MAIN CREDIT BUREAUS

The ideal approach to manage your credit capably and assume responsibility for your financial circumstance is to be educated. This takes a brief period and exertion on your part. Yet, since your credit scores are crucial to dealing with your accounts and setting aside cash, you must know as much as you can regarding the credit bureaus that formulate credit appraisals. To assist you with getting a running beginning on that strategy's, some details on TransUnion, Experian, and Equifax, the primary credit bureaus of the U.S.:

TransUnion

TransUnion has workplaces the nation over that manage various parts of credit: identity theft, credit management, and other credit issues; and types of credit customers, for example, personal, business, and press inquiries. If you discover errors on your TransUnion credit report, you can call them at 800.916.8800 or visit their site to debate them. If you believe that you are a casualty of identity theft, call them at 800.680.7289 at the earliest opportunity.

Experian

Like other credit bureaus, Experian provides a wide range of various administrations for people, businesses, and the media. Experian is based in Costa Mesa, CA, and has a website. Yet, if you discover errors in your report or need to report potential identity theft, this credit bureau makes it elusive to telephone numbers on the site. Instead, they encourage guests to utilize online forms for questions, identity theft reports, and different issues.

Equifax

Based in Atlanta, GA, Equifax likewise has various departments to help people with multiple types of questions and concerns. Their website is additionally set up to have people utilize online forms to work on errors, report identity theft, and handle different matters. In any case, if somebody believes that their identity has been taken, the individual in question can, however, call 888.397.3742 to report it to Equifax. If somebody detects a blunder on their Equifax credit report, that person must utilize the contact number on the story to question it. There is no number on the site to describe errors.

These are the three credit bureaus in the nation, and they each adopt an alternate strategy to enabling people to get in touch with them to pose inquiries or address any issues they might be encountering. Rather than reaching the credit bureaus legitimately, numerous people prefer to utilize a credit checking administration to assist them with dealing with their credit and stay over their funds. The credit bureaus all have related projects; however, most people prefer to utilize an independent organization to assist them with these issues. That way, they get an impartial perspective on their credit score and many more devices to manage and improve their credit ratings proactively.

Dealing with Credit Bureaus

Today, where the economy is at its weak point, having good credit is a necessary tool. This is because it allows you to obtain house loans, car loans, credit cards, and other convenient financial services and instruments. You may be able to live without having good credit. You can discern the credit bureau that holds your file by looking at any rejection letter you received from a recent credit application. If you are dealing with the credit bureau that handles your data, keep in mind that it belongs in the business of collecting and selling information. As such, you should not provide them with any detail, which is not necessarily legal. When you already have your credit report, make sure to check for any errors or discrepancies. If you find anything questionable in your story, you can send the credit bureau a written request for them to investigate the failure. In general, the credit bureau has the burden of documenting anything included in your credit report. If the credit bureau fails to investigate the error or neglects your request for an investigation within 30 days, the error should be removed. You need to educate yourself about credit bureaus' legal obligations to have a successful credit repair process. Before dealing with them, make sure you know all the legal aspects to not end up paying for something that should not be charged with a fee. Remember, credit bureaus are also businesses and that they own many credit repair companies.

Making the Best of Credit Bureaus

It is a little annoying to learn that all three credit bureaus have sensitive financial data. However, there is no method to prevent lenders and collection entities from sharing your information with the above companies. You can limit any possible problems associated with the credit bureaus by evaluating your credit reports annually and acting immediately if you notice some errors. It is also good to monitor your credit cards and other open credit products to ensure that no one misuses the accounts. If you have a card that you do not often use, sign up for alerts on that card so that you get notified if any transactions happen and regularly review statements for your active tickets. Next, if you notice any signs of fraud or theft, you can choose to place a credit freeze with the three credit bureaus and be diligent in tracking your credit card's activity in the future.

How the Bureaus Get Their Information

To learn how the score gets calculated, we need to learn about your score's different inputs, aka where the bureaus get their info. You may have many factors that report information to the credit bureaus or none. Credit cards are called revolving accounts or revolving debt by the credit bureaus. Each monthly payment and balance are reported, as well as any late payments. This means that any cards that have your name on them will also report to all the bureaus. This includes cards that belong to a spouse or parent. If you are an authorized user on the account, it gets reported on your credit no matter what. Many people have their credit ruined by a spouse or parent going into bankruptcy or not paying their credit card bills. If your name is on any credit card that belongs to people that may not pay their bills, ask them to take your name off immediately! Installment loans also report information to the credit bureaus. If you went down to your local Sears and financed a washer/dryer set by putting up a down payment, that is an installment loan. The details of these loans are all reported; the total balance, as well as the timeliness and amounts of your monthly payments. If you have mortgages or student loans, that information does get reported. Total amounts due, total paid so far, and the status of monthly payments is all reported. This information is kept track of and organized in their databases.

14. REMOVING BAD RECORDS

Many people face mistakes in their reports. It has even been estimated that about one-fifth of consumers have found errors in their reports from one of the three major credit bureaus. Less likely but still far too common is when an error on your report causes you to get bad loans or insurance rates. About one in twenty people have lost money due to mistakes.

Viewing these odds makes it all the more important for you to understand your credit report and how to fix any mistakes. The chances are that it could happen to you or someone you know.

Mistakes could be accounts that are not yours, wrong amounts, or false claims of account delinquency. If anything like this is on your report, you need to file a dispute. Otherwise, it will remain on your record and cause you and your score harm.

You may have noticed that each credit report you receive will come with a web address for the credit bureaus' online dispute forms. These forms are fine to use but are not as effective as sending written correspondence, especially if your report's error is a major problem. Although you are free to use their online services, the reasons why using a letter is the better method are explained in more detail below.

The FCRA requires credit bureaus to investigate any dispute you make and respond to you within 30 days of the dispute. This time limit is extended to 45 days if you provide more information regarding the dispute during this period. You can see that the item(s) being disputed are under investigation on your credit report as they are marked as disputed until a resolution has been made or the information is proven to be accurate.

If the credit bureaus' decision is not satisfactory or you find your case being handled carelessly, you should file a complaint at the company. You can do this online with the Consumer Financial Protection Bureau and with the company in question. You can also request that the fact that you filed a dispute and it was not resolved to your satisfaction be noted on all of your future credit reports. That statement can be sent to those who have seen your report before the change.

Being denied insurance, credit, or employment or being given bad credit terms based on the information that is in your credit report is not an ideal situation. So, what can you do about it? First of all, if that happened to you, you should have received a notification from the insurance company, lender, or employer with the credit bureau's contact information that they used for the information to make the decision.

Within sixty days of receiving this notice, you are legally entitled to a free report from that credit bureau. If there is an error that influenced the decision, you can dispute both the error with the credit bureau and the company that provided the credit bureau with the information. If the error has caused damages, you can seek compensation in court.

When your dispute investigation is completed, you will also receive a written notice of the results from where you filed your dispute. If your information was indeed inaccurate, all three of the nationwide credit bureaus would also be notified to correct their information if necessary. You will also be entitled to another free credit report if the dispute results in a change to its information. Additionally, if any information is removed or changed, a credit bureau cannot include it in your report again unless it is verified to be correct and complete.

If any information on your report changes, you can request that a copy with the notice of any corrections that were made be sent to any person or company that saw your report within the last six months. For employment, anyone who received your report within two years before the change can be sent a copy and notification as well.

Removing Late Payments, Charge-offs, and Collections

Late payments, charge-offs, and collections all harm your credit substantially and should be dealt with in some way.

 Late payments tend to become charge-offs and then go to collections, so dealing with your late payments first is a good idea. How you decide to deal with your late payments depends a lot on your general credit history and your history with the company you are late with.

First of all, you should understand how late payments, charge-offs, and collections affect your credit. The longer they are past due, the most important factor is not how much the payment is worth. Taking this into consideration can prevent a majority of your late payments. Say you have three payments due but only enough money to cover either the two smaller or one larger amount. Knowing your credit is affected by the time and number of accounts past due, you should logically pay the two smallest accounts first, preventing at least one late payment.

You should also note that your late payment will not automatically be reported. Depending on the situation, it will take a minimum of 30 days to show up on your credit report and might not show at all until you close the account. Unless you are late by at least 30 days, it will not show up at all. Also, know that even if you pay off a late payment, charge-off, or collection, it will still show up in your credit report unless you do something else about it.

If you are 90 days late, it can be turned into a charge-off, but you can still play if you are that late to avoid charge-offs, collections, and even repossessions.

Some good methods to achieving this are not dispute letters. They are either requesting a goodwill adjustment from your creditor or offering to sign up for automatic payments. A goodwill adjustment is a good option for those with a good history. What you do is send a letter that asks the creditor to forgive a late payment in a way that explains how you have been a good client, what went wrong, and why you would like to have the record removed.

Another option is to sign up for automatic payments. This can work, even if you have been a repeat offender with late payments but will likely only remove your most recent late payment. This works because you give the creditor a more concrete commitment to pay on time in the future. You have to make sure that the money is in your checking account when scheduled to be withdrawn, so you might find that this is not a good choice.

Probably the best way to remove late payments is with a letter which will be explained further below.

As for charge-offs, you should first consider if it would be better to use your time and money to just pay it off. It will still show up in your report this way but will be less of a blemish than if it is left unpaid. You should pay a charge-off if it is recent, if you are trying to qualify for a home loan, if you have an agreement with the creditor for it to be deleted or re-aged if you pay it. You should not pay a charge-off if it is listed for multiple companies; you do not know if you owe the amount shown or if it is past the statute of limitations.

Any negotiations you do with the company holding your charge-off can be done over the phone, but like most things involving credit, it is best to do it all in writing to have physical records.

While it might be harder to remove collections from your credit report, it can still be done. Review the rules in the FCRA and your state for the statutes of limitations and the timeline you have to work with before starting the process of removing collections since they are the most sensitive to work with, and you could inadvertently harm your credit in the long run. Many people find this too difficult and seek professional help, but that is not always necessary. Choose the route that is best for you.

Accounts that remain unpaid for four to six months, depending on the company, get sent to collections. You might not be contacted about your debt during this time. That is a signal that you need to do something about the debt. People often get caught off-guard by nasty collection calls and letters if they do not remember or understand their debt.

Unlike late payments and charge-offs, paying your collections account will not improve your credit score. So, take that into account with your negotiations. Also, make sure that you still owe the collection since debt buyers will buy your debt for less than it was originally worth, and the statute of limitations might be over.

Send a validation request to the collection agency listed on your credit report to confirm that they own the debt and start correspondence. They have to send you the proof in writing that they do own your debt and if you still owe it.

Do not pay on debt in collections unless you know the statute of limitations and the reporting date. If you pay on an account, it will re-age it, making it stay on your credit report longer than necessary. If you are coerced into paying without knowing this information, it is illegal under the FCRA, and you should seek legal counsel. You might even be open to a lawsuit which can lead to a judgment on the account.

If you try these other methods and they do not work or are not suitable for your situation, you can send a dispute letter directly to the credit bureau. You can only do this if some of the information is incorrect or unverifiable. Otherwise, it will not be removed.

Comb through your records to locate any information such as the dates, payment amounts, and any other pertinent information that is correct on your credit report. If you find anything, you can file a dispute by sending a dispute letter to all credit bureaus that list the incorrect information. If they cannot verify the information, it must be removed from your report, which could have entire negative records removed for you if it works in your favor.

15. IMPORTANCE OF GOOD CREDIT SCORE

These days, society is increasingly dependent on credit scores when it comes to making a wide variety of different decisions about your future. As such, if your credit isn't as good as you might like, it will affect more than just your rates on loan or if you are eligible for a credit card. Your credit is essentially a history that shows how strict you have been when it comes to reliably pay bills on time in the past, which means a wide variety of different individuals are going to be curious about it as a way of determining how you are likely to act in the future.

Your credit score can vacillate from 350, indicating you are an extremely high-risk investment, to 850, which indicates anyone who loans you money is almost certain to get it back. Additionally, your credit rating is typically shown via a numerical rating from 1 (very bad) to 9 (very good). Currently, only about five percent of Americans have a credit rating of 500 or lower, while about fifteen percent have a score above 800, with the majority falling between the 700 and 800 range.

Living arrangements

First and foremost, your credit score affects your ability to get a mortgage and what you will pay monthly and overall. A poor credit rating can also prevent you from successfully getting a mortgage at all, or even prevent landlords from renting to you as well. This is because many landlords consider a lease a type of loan; after all, they are loaning you're a place to live in exchange for rent each month.

Car payments

The quality of your credit will also affect whether you will be approved for a loan for the car you are interested in purchasing, as well as what your interest rate is going to be. In this case, bad credit can limit your options as fewer lenders will be willing to work with you, and those that do are generally going to charge more to balance out the risk you represent. This typically translates into repayments for longer periods (72 months instead of 60 or less) and higher overall payments each month.

Job search: While the first two scenarios are expected, many people will be surprised to learn that a low credit score can affect your employment prospects. While employers can't check credit scores, they can check credit reports, and many do so as a routine part of the hiring process. Depending on the job, if you have a history of poor financial responsibility, an employer may be hesitant to offer you the position you have been dreaming about. Likewise, many companies check credit reports to ensure their executives won't give the company a bad name when it comes to promotions.

Starting a business

Those who are grinding away at a 9-to-5 aren't the only ones who need to worry about their credit score; if you are self-employed, a negative credit score can have even more serious implications. If you are looking to start a business with a small business loan, then you can bet lenders will check your credit score and, as most new businesses tend to fail, they will be very selective about who they lend their money to.

Monthly bills

Your credit score will also affect many of your monthly bills, including your utilities. Utility companies loan you their services every month, and if your credit report shows that you are a risky investment, then they will most definitely charge you more for the privilege of having electricity, running water, cellular service, or cable and internet.

16. TIPS AND TRICKS FOR SUCCESS WITH SECTION 609

Whether you would like to delete only one thing from your record otherwise, you are looking to delete tons of various things at an equivalent time. You would like to make sure that your 609 Letter is taken care of and prepared to go. There are tons of parts that take to go through to get this done, but once you check out a number of the templates that we, you'll see that this is often not as bad because it could be.

It's necessary to write out a number of the letters you would like to send to the credit agencies, and you're getting all of the documentation able to go, confirm to follow a number of the overall advice that we have below:

Keep All of the Records

Everything has to be recorded on your end of things. Don't just send a letter then assume that it will be all good. You never know when things will go missing or once you will have to prove your side of things. The more accurate and in-depth records you're ready to take, the higher it'll be with everyone.

This means that we'd like to stay track of everything, from the instant that we start sending out information and letters to the credit bureaus until way after the very fact once they take that information off your credit report. This may assist you if anything comes back afterward. Otherwise, you have to confirm that you can prove your side of the story if the credit agency doesn't respond or do what they're alleged to.

Keep track of everything that you simply can along the way. You ought to have all of the letters you send, both the originals and any follow-ups you send. If the credit agency gets back in-tuned with you, then you ought to keep the letters they send to you and your responses around. You'll hold onto all of the supporting documents that you send. The more information you increase your records about this, the higher it'll be to get your way in the process.

Add-In the Identification Information

Before you send any information or work with section 609, confirm that you send alongside it some identification information. This will confirm that the credit agency will know who you're and prove that they're working with the one that says they own the account or at least own the SSN that goes with all that information on the credit report.

There are tons of various options that you are ready to use to show your identity, and you ought to include a variety of them together with your letter to help prove who you're. You'd want to work with information like your driver's license, Social Security numbers, and more to showcase who you're and why you would like to make a difference in the credit report.

Consider Bringing Something Up, Albeit It Doesn't Look Important

While you're at this process, it's worth mentioning even a number of the smaller things on your report. Albeit these don't look important at the time, and that they aren't the most thing you want to place some time and a spotlight is, while you're writing the letter, you ought to add in as many details and as many disputes that are legitimate as possible.

You never know what you'd be ready to get erased off the credit report and the way much of a difference that will make to your credit score along the way. Albeit the item seems small, you ought to consider adding it to the dispute that you will do.

Sometimes, the deadline will continue too long, and therefore the agency won't respond. If this happens, all of the things, whether or not they are big or small, will have to be taken out of the report. And you'll find that even a couple of small things can add up to be big things at the end of the day. Although the credit agency won't erase all of the small things, it doesn't take much of a difference along the way when you simply fancy catch on all done. And it could make a difference.

Do Not Contact The FTC

One thing that tons of individuals will attempt to use is to contact the FTC and other agencies in the hope of getting things fixed. They'll hope that because there's something wrong with the credit report, the FTC will be ready to help them look out for this. Sometimes they're mad and need to get the agency in trouble for falsely adding things to their reports. And other times, they'll not know who they're alleged to contact.

However, this is often not getting to does one any good. If you contact the FTC, they won't provide you with the help that you need. Their stance is that they're not getting to get in between you and the credit agency in the least, and everyone you'll revisit is a letter stating these facts. Since you have other options at your disposal, you do not have to work with the FTC but confirm that you will not waste time in the process.

When you want to get something on your credit report fixed and everyone better, it's essential not to waste time with the FTC instead of going straight to the credit agencies. You'll send an equivalent letter and the same information to everyone, and that they are those who are going to be ready to help us to get things done. If you follow the principles that we are using here and a few of the opposite steps, you'll be ready to get your credit report taken care of.

Send A Letter to Every Credit Agency

We'd like to recollect here what we have to go through to send out one among these Section 609 letters to every credit agency that we would like to get to get rid of the things. The credit agencies aren't getting to ask each other about this. If you send a letter to Transunion, but to not one among the others, then Transunion may take it off your report, but none of the others would do that for you.

You have to be liable for sending a letter to all or any three of the reporting agencies if you'd wish to get that debt taken out of all of your reports. You ought to automatically send this information to all or any three right from the beginning, so confirm to get copies of all the knowledge so that you're able to go and handle all of that directly.

You can include equivalent information in each of the letters that you send. And you'll even send an identical letter, confirm to vary the corporate and department name that you simply are using on all. Then include an equivalent proof of your identity, the credit reports, and more for everyone to get the ball rolling here.

Mention Section 609 in the Letter

We'd like to recollect a couple of various things when it involves writing out our make letters. We'd like to incorporate our name and a few of the knowledge about who we are and where we live. We'd like to include information about the debts and accounts that we might wish to dispute along the way, including a credit report back to show what accounts were talking about. We'd like to make sure that we, at some point, mention section 609 in the letter.

This will be useful in several aspects. First, it will show the credit agency that you know what you're talking about. There are tons of individuals out there who would like to repair their credit scores, but they don't understand the laws, or they're trying to sneak things past. The credit agencies will notice these individuals easily and cannot want to work with them in the least.

But once you undergo and mention Section 609 in your letter, like we've talked about thus far in this guidebook, then you'll find that it's much easier for you to grab their attention. You have done your research, you recognize what your rights are, and you're able to take them on to get the credit report taken care of. The credit agencies will notice and respect this, which will make it more likely that they're going to hear you and send the knowledge that you need or erase the knowledge that ought not to be there.

Mention the 30-Day Limit

In addition to creating sure that you mention Section 609 in the letter you send, you would also like to confirm that you mention the 30 days that the agency gets to reply to you. This not only helps to point out that you have an honest idea about what you're talking of here but will make it easier for you to remind the credit agency about this right that you have with Section 609 that we mention here.

The letters below will have samples of how you're ready to write these calls in your letter. But confirm to say this which you expect the credit agency to reply and work thereupon deadline to get things taken care of. If you do this, it's tons harder for them to return with not knowing about the deadline, and sets out an equivalent expectation that everybody on each side must follow.

Use one among the Templates you recognize where to start.

You would like to make sure that you write it call correctly, that you mention the right parts about Section 609, and you would like to make sure that you sound such as you know what you're talking about along the way.

The good news is that we've provided some templates that we are ready to use to take care of this process. There are several Section 609 templates that you are ready to work with at the top of this guidebook, and that they are going to be ready to provide you with the proper way to word your letters to get them noticed. They're going to mention Section 609, the FCRA, and even the 30-day notice that's important so that you'll write out a letter that's getting to get noticed and may assist you to wash out your credit report.

Send a Follow-Up Letter

We might imagine that each of the work is completed and that we won't need to do anything after we send off the initial letter to all or any three credit agencies. But unfortunately, there are a couple of other steps that we'd like to finish. Once you're confident that the 30 days have passed and you've given the corporate enough time to reply to what you sent in, it's time to send the follow-up letter telling them that it's now their responsibility to get rid of that information from your credit report.

We will provide you with an honest template that you can use at the top of this guidebook for the follow-up letter. But it basically will tell the agency you sent in information about the various disputes you had on your credit report. Since they need not reply in the timely manner given by the FRCA in Section 609, it's now time for them to get rid of those items from your credit report.

17. CONSEQUENCES OF NOT PAYING OFF YOUR DEBT

What happens when you go into serious defaults on your loans?

Well, it depends on the type of loan. With cars and houses, they can be repossessed by the bank. With consumer debt, you will often have to declare bankruptcy to wipe out old debts if you are far enough underwater.

Government-backed student loans, however, are a whole different beast. They can NOT be removed via bankruptcy. After 270 days of no payments, they are officially in default and sit there like a bad acne breakout on your credit report, making your score look yucky. Some student loan companies will then turn the loans over to official debt collection companies, starting yammering your phone away about late payments. In addition, you'll be on the hook for their own special fees. Yay.

You might have to try the 'secured credit card' trick to build up your credit again after this kind of financial disaster. Some people want to reach out to a debt settlement company or try to get a payday loan, but please don't! Debt settlement companies have to get paid too, you know, and they'll come after your money one way or another. Most of them are scams. The only honest ones are nonprofits, and even those are doubtful. Payday loans charge sickening interest rates of more than 500% in some cases, so for a $1,000 payday loan, you'll be screwed out of more than $5,000. What kind of sense does that make? Stay far away from them.

If you don't pay your credit cards, they sit untouched with the original creditor for about six months. An original creditor is a bank like Chase, Citi, Capital One, Discover, or American Express. If you keep making payments, even if it's just $10 a month, the account will remain open with the original creditor.

But if you stop making payments for six months, then the original creditor turns the debt along with its collected interest over to a debt collection company. They then attempt to collect the debt for another six months. By now, you've not made a single payment for a year. If no payments are made, then your debt, with any added fees and other expenses from the debt collection company, is then turned over to a law office, where a judgment is brought against you in the form of a lawsuit. The law office represents either the original creditor or the debt buying company. The amount of small claims lawsuits based on collecting past debts has increased significantly in the past ten years, and now there are specialty law firms devoted solely to debt collecting from ordinary people. Well, at least we don't have debtors' prisons anymore.

If this happens, the creditor or debt collector is the plaintiff, and you become the defendant. You can even go to trial and meet with a lawyer to set up court-ordered payment plans based on the actual financial paperwork that you bring to the courthouse. Keep in mind that there is often interest included even after judgment is brought against you.

If you still fail to pay, a lien could be put on your property, and your wages could be garnished from your current paycheck. It's legal in most states to garnish up to 25% of your wages. However, if you are seriously buried, you should know that the great state of Texas does not allow wage garnishment, so if you are considering a move, Texas might be the place!

Being informed about this entire process will help you make better decisions on repairing your credit before bills go to collections. Dealing with debt collectors is its own game, so let's take a look. It's a bit different than just dealing with a credit card company. The rules have changed.

Make Debt Collectors Go Away

Unfortunately, debt collector companies just won't take your word for it that you're going through a rough time or that they need to leave you alone. They do need to see proof. Collectors love paperwork! The more proof in writing, the better. So, before calling up your debt collector to give them the complete story of why you can't pay, get yourself prepared.

Spend the time gathering up all of your financial paperwork. Get copies of your taxes that show your income and your financial situation. Gather your doctor's bills, your SSDI paperwork, your paystubs, and, if you're sharing an income or living on someone else's SSI, all the paperwork goes along with that person.

Then, once you've gathered all your paperwork, call up your collector. Keep an eye on the prompts on the phone until you get to the customer service department. Be prepared to wait a long time on the phone. Just set aside the time to devote to this. Be polite but brief and direct. Tell the representative that you can't pay and you have the proof you can't. Ask them how you can get them the paperwork so they can attach it to your file. Maybe you can send it in an email as a PDF attachment or mail it or fax it to them? Get the name of the representative and the state (or country) where they are. Take down your account number. Ask if you need to provide any other paperwork as proof of the inability to pay. If they tell you that you need something, comply with that. Ask if they can put a financial hardship status on your account. If so, that's great. Many collectors don't.

After you hang up, immediately follow the representative's instructions to send the paperwork to the collector. Keep all originals and only send copies. After two weeks, call up the customer service department again. Explain that you spoke to "Name," and have they received all of your paperwork? Make sure every last piece of paper is attached to your file.

The third step is to put your name on their "Do Not Call" list. VERY IMPORTANT: Keep in mind that they won't call about important stuff, either, like courtesy calls notifying you that your balance has changed. So, do this with caution. Yes, the phone calls are uber annoying. But that's the primary legal way of contacting you.

You actually need to send your request not to be contacted in writing. Write or type legibly on a blank sheet of paper:

To Capital One,

Please put my name on your "Do Not Call" list. Please remove my name from all call lists. I understand that I will not receive any phone calls.

Thank you,

Your Name

Keep a copy in case you need it for legal purposes. After you've mailed your request to the collector, wait three weeks for them to receive it and attach the request to your file. Your account will be flagged "Do Not Call" if it's been done properly. Follow up and call the collector to make sure your account has been flagged. Ask the representative if you need to do anything else to make sure you are not contacted.

Throughout this whole negotiating process, continue to send what payments you can. Yes, you can absolutely send small payments to a debt collector, even if it's just $10 or $20 a month. It buys you a little time to change your financial situation. Don't give up, and don't just stop sending payments.

You can also settle with debt collectors. Ask them about settlement options and start with less than 50% of the debt owed. They might come back with a counter-offer. After you agree to the settlement, stick with its terms to the letter, or you will be on the hook for the whole amount, and you can't renegotiate for a new settlement. If you do this, make sure you have them put Paid in Full on your credit report if possible.

18.   REBUILD YOUR CREDIT

Credit card debts are probably seen as something that causes great distress. Apart from rebuilding your credit history, your mentality should be focused on getting out of debt and building wealth. Dumping debt is empowering. And you have the power to stay out of debt if you really want to.

The following is added information on how you can rebuild your credit and finally proclaim yourself debt-free.

Use Good Credit to Leverage Your Way Up

If you have gone through a bad experience with credit cards, you would probably associate the word "credit" with the word "bad." Good credit breeds good credit. Part of the technique is to use your credit and be wise enough to become a person of good standing. With a good credit rating, you can get the best interest rates on your loans and credit cards. Having good credit standing helps you become more aware of your status and keep to it. Collection calls are now a thing of the past. The constant feeling of worrying about how to settle your monthly dues is no longer a major concern. Bills are paid off, and you feel a certain kind of control, freedom, and peace of mind.

There Needs to Be an Activity and Constant Update

In order to rebuild your credit, do not let old information sit for a long time. Your credit report should always have recent activities listed for at least six months. Be active and generate good information. There has to be a timely and consistent pattern of payments so you can be flagged for consistent payments. Having regular activity means your credit report gets fresh updates every month.

Get a Secured Credit Card

This is another way to prove that you are credit-worthy. If getting a regular credit card is not possible, you may get a secured card. It works in a way that you deposit a certain amount in the bank, and in essence, allow you to borrow it back. Your credit limit depends on the money that you have deposited. Pay your monthly fees on time and request a regular card after a year of no delay payments. Finally, the more important part is that you confirm with the credit union if they turn in your good standing information to the credit reporting agencies. Remember your purpose in getting the card – build your credit rating. So if they are not going to turn up on the credit report, this whole thing of rebuilding your credit is pointless.

Borrow a Small Installment Loan from Your Trusted Bank

This is another way towards a stellar credit report. It may seem odd at first but know that credit scores are calculated based on having different kinds of loans and not just credit cards. You can just opt to borrow a small amount from the bank and keep the length of the loan for at least a year. The goal is to establish a new credit path and regularly spark your credit score.

Co-Sign a Loan with Someone

Just a word of caution: co-sign a loan with someone whom you know is responsible enough to take on debt and pay for it. Remember, when you co-sign, you share the debt. And, if they fail to repay the debt, the lending bank will come to you for full payment. Also, if your spouse or a family member is an authorized user of your credit card, you can make him/her a joint account holder. Getting credit under each person's name can give you good credit.

Completely Eliminate Your Debt for Life

If there is one method that would cure your debts and worries away, that would have to be debt elimination. You can do this by allotting money meant for your bills. Or, if you have saved up for the rainy days, now is the time to take that out and lessen your debts. Paying them could save you hundreds and thousands of dollars on interest rates. You would not want to pay high-interest rates for life, don't you?

Apply the Debt Reduction Method

All you have to do is prepare a simple draft of your income statement showing your net worth, a balance sheet, and two letters from your CPA. Showing concrete statements is one of your most powerful tools in reducing your debt drastically. Just do not forget to consult your financial adviser about this.

Always Check for Identity Theft

There is a high probability that there could be an unexplained item (s) in your credit report that does not belong to you. The sad fact is that it is a bad credit score. If this happens, you could be denied credit, and you are going to pay for it. So if there is something mysterious that you see in your credit report, call the credit card company immediately. You need to act fast because you could be a victim of identity theft. It is a real threat.

Avoid becoming a victim by following these safety tips:

- Do not disclose any personal information over the phone, such as your social security number and credit card number.
- Almost all thefts occur online, so be smart when doing your online banking. Always log off your account once finished.
- Change your password regularly.
- Run an antivirus or security software all the time.
- Do not use online banking when on a Wi-Fi network in public places.

Be Wiser When Handling Finances

You have probably learned your lesson the hard way. But what is important is that you learn from it and act on it. This way, you will not fall victim to this scrupulous scheme again and somehow learn how to play this tricky game.

19. HOW TO INCREASE YOUR CREDIT LIMIT

Increasing your credit limit is an easy way to improve your credit score – if you do it right.

A credit card does not have to be something you keep in the back of your pocket for emergencies only. Indeed, with the abundance of credit cards that allow you to collect rewards ranging from cash to airline miles, your credit card can be a fantastic financial tool. However, if you opened your account right after graduating from college or when your credit was less than stellar, you do not have a very high spending cap. The good news is that you can request a credit limit raise. But first, learn how to raise your credit limit without harming your credit score.

How Your Credit Limit Influences Your Credit Score

Your credit limit does not affect your credit score on its own, but how you use it does. Your credit limit reflects the amount of credit you have available to you. It doesn't have much of an effect on its own, but the amount you owe reflects your utilization, which can be very significant.

The total amount of revolving credit you owe divided by the total amount of credit extended to you yields your credit usage. For example, if you have a credit card with a $1,000 limit and a $100 balance, your credit utilization ratio is 10%. However, if you bill an additional $500, the usage rises to 60%.

Credit scores consider both your utilization rate on of credit card and your average credit utilization across all accounts.

A reasonable rule of thumb is to keep the utilization rate below 30% at all times. The lower your usage rate, however, the better. A high credit utilization rate may indicate financial distress, while a low credit utilization rate indicates that you're using less of your available credit.

Credit rating models can perceive low utilization as a sign that you're doing a good job handling your credit and controlling your spending. Credit usage is an important factor to remember since it accounts for 30% of your overall FICO ranking.

How to Raise Your Credit Limit and Raise Your Credit Score

While many people are suspicious of ways they can inadvertently harm their credit scores, increasing your credit limit is a simple way to increase your score.

Increasing your credit limit reduces your usage instantly. Take, for example, the preceding example. If you raised your credit card limit from $1,000 to $2,000 while leaving your $600 balance alone, your usage would fall from 60% to 30%. This may have a huge impact on your overall ranking.

Of course, this only works if your balances are poor. "For some people, higher credit limits can reflect the temptation to spend more," Griffin says. If your spending exceeds your credit cap, you will not benefit from a higher credit limit. In reality, if you're not careful, you could end up increasing your utilization ratio.

In general, paying down your credit card balance and keeping it as low as possible is the best way to increase your utilization ratio.

While requesting a credit limit increase is generally beneficial to your credit, it will temporarily lower your score. This is because credit card companies will sometimes conduct a hard pull on your credit to ensure you meet their requirements for a higher cap.

When considering a higher credit cap request, each card issuer has its own set of conditions. Some lenders will look at your credit report before approving any rise, while others will not.

However, the effect is minor. Hard credit pulls usually lower your credit score by five to ten points and remain on your credit report for two years.

How to Request a Credit Line Expansion

If you're ready for a credit limit boost, your card issuer might have already issued you one. It's not uncommon for credit card companies to raise credit limits regularly as a reward for spending regularly but responsibly and paying the bills on time. However, many large credit card companies will not automatically increase your credit limit until you have made at least six to twelve months of on-time payments and have not surpassed your credit limit in the past.

If you haven't got an automatic raise, most of the time, all you have to do is inquire. Creditors usually do not mind-expanding credit lines.

In reality, if they think you would use it and pay for it, they will welcome it.

Many credit card companies allow you to make the request online. Simply log in to your account, change your income records, and receive an instant response. In most situations, you'll need to dial the number on the back of your card and speak with a customer service representative.

The measures for requesting a credit line increase from major credit card issuers are as follows:

Bank of America

Cardholders of Bank of America can request an increase in their credit limit by calling customer service at 800-732-9194 or logging into the issuer's online banking service. If your account is eligible for a credit line increase, you can request one online by selecting your credit card account, clicking the "details & services" tab, and then clicking the "credit line increase" connection in the "manage your account" section of "services." The connection will not appear if you are not entitled to request a Bank of America credit line increase.

Capital One

Capital One cardholders can request an increase in their credit limit by calling 877-383-4802 or applying online. Begin by choosing your card account when requesting a credit line increase online. Capital One will then request that you enter or confirm personal information such as your annual income, job status, monthly mortgage or rent payment, and preferred maximum credit line. Often Capital One will accept the new limit immediately, while other times, it can take up to a few days. In this case, Capital One will send a letter outlining the decision's specifics.

Chase

Chase cardholders can request an increase in their credit limit by calling customer support at 800-432-3117 or sending a safe message online. Log into your online banking account, select "connect with Chase" from the main menu, and then "secure messages" to request a Chase credit line increase. Include your gross annual income, total credit line request, housing status, and monthly housing payment sum in your letter. Chase will then review your data and respond with a safe response.

Discover

Credit line increases can be requested by calling customer service at 800-347-2683 or by logging into online banking and making the request online. To request a Discover credit limit increase online, go to the top menu and select "manage," then click the "credit line increase" link. You'll then be directed to a page that displays your current card information, including your current credit limit and the amount of credit you have available. Enter your total annual gross income, your employer's name, and your monthly housing cost here, then press "send." Residents of Ohio and New York and joint applicants are unable to make a request online and must call to request a credit limit increase.

If you've been making just the minimum payments or your balance has been slowly might month after month, your lender could be worried, as these may be viewed as indicators of financial distress. If this is the case, you can postpone requesting a credit limit increase until you've paid off your balance or got a raise.

If you are refused a rise, you should consider opening a new card instead."

The practices of various lenders vary. One may be attempting to restrict credit, while another may be attempting to extend it.

Avoiding Pitfalls When Requesting a Credit Line Increase

In principle, increasing your credit limit should improve your credit score overall. However, the state of your credit is determined by how you treat your account. Be certain that you do not undo the progress you've made by making mistakes with your credit.

Missing a payment is the worst thing you can do to your credit score. Payment history is the most critical credit score aspect, accounting for 35% of your FICO score. Missing even one bill payment will dramatically lower your credit score.

Breaking your routine is the second-worst thing you can do. When it comes to improvements to the financial condition, it's better to slow down and make deliberate decisions. Too many changes at once, such as several credit requests in a short time, can harm your credit score. Apply for new credit only when you really need it.

When it comes to can your credit cap, think about your overall financial picture first. For example, if you know you're a big spender, it may not be a good idea to request a raise because it might lead to more debt and damage your credit scores.

On the other hand, if you have a strong grasp on your finances and can keep balances low, increasing your credit limit may be the secret to expanding your financial options.

20. CONCLUSION

You should now have a better idea of repairing your credit with or without using section 609. While many people feel that this is one of the best ways to get rid of your bad credit, there are many situations where writing a dispute letter will not help you gain better credit. For example, if you have missed payments on your credit cards within a certain amount of time. Even if the credit card company states that you didn't pay during the months you did, this is something that won't work to dispute because you have recently missed payments.

In the times we live in, it is almost impossible to live without having at least one credit. The unstable unemployment rates can affect everyone, so more and more Americans are confronted with bad credit. You have to understand that bad credit gets even worse over time as its grave consequences will be felt more and more, leading to things such as the impossibility to get new credit, refinance an old credit, rent an apartment, or get a job. This is why you should act in a time and take care of your finances, especially in the context of a shaky national and international economy.

When it comes to struggling with credit card debt, the best way to start repairing your credit is to make sure you understand the federal laws associated with credit card debt. Be assured that you have been protected and that the credit card company is not doing anything illegally. If everything is legal, then you simply want to work on paying off your credit card payments.

You will want to develop a financial plan that will help you start to pay off your debt strategically. You then want to make sure that, no matter what, you follow this plan. Even if you find yourself in an emergency after a few months when your car breaks down, you want to find another way to come up with your emergency funding. You must continue to make more than the minimum payment on time with all your credit cards. The fewer fees you need to add to your balance, the quicker you will be able to pay off your credit card debt.

While many people don't realize this, most credit card companies want to work with you. The number one reason for this is they want to keep you as a customer, basically, so they can continue receiving your money. One strategy to use is to call and say that you would like to close your account. They will then try to focus on keeping your account open, resulting in them dropping a few missed payments or over the limit fees. Another strategy to use is simply to explain to them what happened, why you were late, and tell them that you want to put your account in good standing. They are usually willing to drop some fees or so much money if you are willing to pay a certain amount off that day.

Remember to be consistent and make sure to rid yourself of all the unnecessary expenses that you have. Try to establish a new and fresh way to keep track of your payments. Do not be afraid to act, for it is only then that you will be able to see the result. Always think positive, and do not let failure hold you back from your goal to be creditworthy once again. In the end, all the efforts are truly worth it. Not only will you have peace of mind and feel better about your life, but the more important goal is to have a trouble-free process in acquiring a new house or car because of your good and trustworthy credit. What is more, you might even land the job or start the business that you have been dreaming of because of that good credit standing. Isn't that something to look forward to?

Suppose you decide to write a dispute letter under section 609 because you have noticed that information that reflects negatively on your credit score is over seven years old. In that case, you should follow the tips and guidelines. You want to make sure that you do your best when writing this letter. Don't feel that it is just a simple letter and write it quickly. Ensure that you have all the information you need, all the documentation, proofread the letter and certify the letter with a receipt request. Keep all the correspondence you receive and send, keep your original copies, and anything else. You want to have a thorough paper trail.

You also have a set budget which you follow every month. This includes ways to increase your emergency fund, so you can think about safely closing your last credit card account and no longer even have credit cards on your mind. With every credit card offer you receive in the mail, you immediately shred and then recycle the paper.

You are living comfortably and growing your savings. You have finally reached financial freedom.

"Creditors have better memories than debtors."
-Benjamin Franklin

Lightning Source UK Ltd.
Milton Keynes UK
UKHW022034280521
384576UK00002B/314